AUGUST
STRINDBERG

AUGUST STRINDBERG

A Study by
L. LIND–AF–HAGEBY

Comprising a lecture delivered before the
Anglo-Swedish Society on December 6th, 1927,
at which Mr. Robert Loraine took the Chair.

Introductory Note by
ROBERT LORAINE

KENNIKAT PRESS
Port Washington, N. Y./London

AUGUST STRINDBERG

First published in 1928
Reissued in 1970 by Kennikat Press
Library of Congress Catalog Card No: 76-103201
SBN 8046-0838-5

Manufactured by Taylor Publishing Company   Dallas, Texas

AUGUST STRINDBERG.
Bust by CARL ELDH.
Reproduced by kind permission of the Sculptor.

INTRODUCTORY NOTE.

AUGUST STRINDBERG is little known in England.

Yet he should be as established as Euclid, and as legendary as King Arthur.

For the voice that rings out through his work touches the same truth as the law of Euclid, and is part of the Universal Law: and the oppression he labours under and seeks to relieve is as great as the darkness and yoke of the dragons of yore.

For it is the pall of untruth.

His life depicts a struggle, an aim and an achievement as varied, as mighty, as romantic and as world-resounding as the combats of the Round Table.

He took on the woes of the people, he sought redress and tried to shatter a way to the truth: but victory was elusive, for the monsters he attacked were not outlying foes, but the worms that lie at the very heart of life, around the core of man, in the injustice and the torments we mete out to each other and inflict on ourselves.

What was the purpose, the end, the cause of the vagaries and the tricks of life?

He sought to know.

Only a transmuted echo of his struggles reaches us, and because of that transmutation and because of the misunderstanding that attends and clouds every new manifestation of the creative and visionary force in man, his work has been misconstrued; he is referred to as " the crazy genius," " the emissary of hate," and he is thought to be mad.

All seers are mad in the eyes of their generation.

Lest he should escape this present generation, I have tried, and am trying, as far as lies in my power, to show you this vast colossus of mind and of strength that is Strindberg.

He will enlarge your consciousness of life and widen your understanding.

Miss Lind-af-Hageby, who is a woman of letters herself and a recognised authority on Strindberg, will enlighten you regarding the enigma of his work and his life.

ROBERT LORAINE.

AUGUST STRINDBERG

A STUDY

The English play-going public has recently become conscious of the existence of a number of plays—strong, disturbing, challenging—by a strange Swede, by the name of August Strindberg. This consciousness is largely due to the masterly manner in which one of Strindberg's characters, *The Father*, has been interpreted by Mr. Robert Loraine. Prior to the year 1927 there had been a certain amount of literary interest in Strindberg and some performances of his dramatic works by the more daring theatrical enterprises. Thus *The Father*, *Lady Julie*, *The Creditors*, *The Stronger*, etc., have been performed before limited audiences. The performance of *The Spook Sonata*, some time ago, produced a certain amount of comment on the weird and whimsical dramatist who could put old ladies in cupboards and make them cry like parrots.

Strindberg died in 1912. All reputations grow or wane. What about his? It has passed through every phase and vicissitude, from detestation to adoration. His writings have been called bad literature, faulty drama, mad, the ripe fruit of supreme genius. Strindberg has been denounced as a sex maniac and hailed as a superman, rising above and beyond the confines of sex. In fact, the appraising of him has ranged from comparisons with

Shakespeare to contempt relegating him to the rôle of a mouldy twig on a heap of rubbish.

To attempt to describe Strindberg's literary output, his work and importance as a dramatist, novelist, essayist, in the space of a lecture* is like attempting to serve up the sea in a thimble.

I once gave a solid ten months to reading and re-reading his books, in an attempt to find his intellectual forbears, his literary inspirers and relations, to find words in which to describe and define him. (Incidentally we may sympathise with Strindberg over the misfortune that anything in the shape of a woman should attempt such a thing!) I found the usual words, categories, definitions utterly inadequate. The ordinary literary label is burst asunder by a writer who, so to speak, incarnates different selves in different forms of art; grows, changes, contradicts himself, excels, fails, attracts, and repels in bewildering succession. His was a multiple personality in which the different selves were at war and yet—strange anomaly—at peace with one another. You can call Strindberg with truth Christian, atheist, sensualist, ascetic, spiritualist, occultist, mystic, scientist, reformer, revolutionary, and conservative. He was always seeking something better. Discontent with what he had found drove him to further search. There was ceaseless movement in his mind.

Fully to describe Strindberg you must be Strindberg. Fully to understand Strindberg you must be what few are—an epitome of humanity, its struggles, weakness and strength, its follies and passions, its

---

* To the lecture have been added passages from *August Strindberg: The Spirit of Revolt*, with the object of making this study more comprehensive. The book mentioned, published in 1913, is now out of print, but will shortly be re-published.

whitest aspirations and blackest hatred. I can think of no one who so completely incarnates himself in his books. You will say that this is true of all who write, for we cannot produce anything—even strange dreams—outside ourselves. But it is not true of other writers in the sense that it is true of Strindberg. The pages of Rousseau, Tolstoy, Flaubert, the great self-confessors of literature, have not the flesh-and-blood reality of Strindberg.

And how are we to understand this strange man?

Let us put ourselves by the mind of a nice, well-educated, well-fed Englishman, an average man interested in drama and fiction, inclined to light biographical studies, tutored to look for pleasant solutions of life's little problems. He knows the place of Shakespeare in the estimation of the world, he admires Barrie and enjoys Bernard Shaw. He has learned that August Strindberg is the author of over 100 works—plays, novels, essays. He wants to know more about him. He has just had a solid Sunday dinner—roast beef and potatoes, Yorkshire pudding and cheese. He summons the ghost of Strindberg (let us suppose he can summon the ghost of Strindberg):

Average Man: Did you write nice plays, plays suitable for the English stage?

Strindberg: That depends on what you think nice. Here's *The Father.* Theme: the terrible power of woman to drive a man insane through making him suspect her fidelity and doubt his paternity.

Average Man: Rather an unpleasant subject.

Strindberg: But true, true. Thousands of men, millions of men have passed through that agony; it is inseparable from the curse of sex.

AUGUST STRINDBERG

Average Man: But better not talked of.

Strindberg: Here is *Lady Julie.* Theme: the
inevitable sex attraction of a weak, neurotic,
aristocratic Miss for the virile son of the people, a
valet who seduces a Countess and seizes a moment
when the oppressed and servile class can get the
better of the tyrannical, insolent upper class.

Average Man: Another unpleasant subject. I say
it is indecent and not suitable for a London theatre.

Strindberg: Yet you have had an extra long run
of such a play as *Our Betters.* If I remember
aright the two culprits return smiling to the stage,
whilst mine give themselves over to the tragedy of
consequences. Your censor permits the performance
of *The Fanatics* and *The Constant Nymph.*

Average Man: Well, they are amusing.

Strindberg (knitting his brows): Amusing? Let
me see: I have *Comrades.* That is a play about a
man-eating woman, the mannish, ambitious, simian-
brained female who intrudes in man's domain, steals
his work, battens on his mind, who, withal, has to
give in in the end to his masculine superiority. Is
not that amusing?

Average Man: No. It is not. We don't write of
women like that.

Strindberg: But have you never *felt* like that?
Have you not opposed women's suffrage and women
Members of Parliament, and—hand on your heart—
would you not hate women bishops or a Cabinet of
women?

Average Man: Well, perhaps. But we don't like
such exaggerated stuff. Let's be reasonable.

Strindberg: There's *Creditors,* showing the erotic woman, the alluring, treacherous, unmoral creature of instinct and passion, the vampire, false, voluptuous and heartless, a coquette, a " mangeuse d'hommes," to whom conjugal monotony is insupportably dull. Her qualities have made Adolf, her husband, a nervous wreck, semi-epileptic. She has been married before, and I show how the imprint of her first husband, soul and body, stands in the way of a union with the second husband. The child turns out to be like the first husband. Do you wonder the second suffers tortures of jealousy and of thwarted love?

Average Man: Another unpleasant play. *Have you nothing pleasant?*

Strindberg: Let me see. Pleasant? Was life pleasant ? There is *Samum,* the story of the revenge of an Arabian girl and her lover on a Frenchman, a Lieutenant in a Zouave regiment. She revenges herself by killing the Frenchman—not with a dagger but by *suggestions* which invoke hideous pictures, making him believe that he has been bitten by a mad dog, that his wife has been faithless, that his child is dead. She murders him by horror.

There are *Crimes and Crimes.* This is another play which I have built around the subtle force of evil thought. Here you see how a child is killed through the hateful thoughts of a man and a woman. He has deserted his child. He left its mother to follow a woman bent on pleasure only. Through a combination of malign circumstances this man is actually accused of having physically murdered his child. Of that he is innocent but not of the evil thought.

(9)

Average Man: Horrible. I prefer the suggestion method of the late Monsieur Coué.

Strindberg: But these things happen. There is *Pariah,* a psychological play in which two respectable rascals are found unmasking one another by one of life's inevitable processes of self-revelation; there is *The Stronger,* a contrast of temperaments between two women, one the wife and the other the mistress of the same man. One speaks, the other woman is silent, but they unmask one another perfectly.

Average Man: Why do you always want to unmask people? We prefer to keep our little illusions.

Strindberg: Then you may like *The First Warning.* This is a play in which a weak, jealous and enslaved husband makes six vain attempts to flee from the charms of his wife. *He* tried to keep his little illusion.

Average Man: Don't be cynical.

Strindberg: That is exactly what I don't want to be. My naturalistic plays—you would call them expressionistic (fashions change)—express my reaction against the *pain* of life; my transcendental plays, my plays of mystery and symbol, express my reaction against the inscrutable fate and mystery of life. I speak of such plays as *To Damascus, Advent, The Dance of Death, Easter, The Crown Bride, Swanwhite, The Dream Play, The Great Highway.* In *Swanwhite* you meet a fairy-like Princess and a chivalrous Prince, romance and roses and springlike innocence. In *Easter* you see an exquisite young girl, pure and lovely. She is what the world calls mad, but all secrets are open to her. She can see the stars during the daytime and hear things that happen far away. She dwells in the realms of pure beauty. In *Advent* you find how ill-treated little children are comforted by the presence of a mysterious playmate clad in white, who brings light to the dark cellar in which they have been imprisoned. *I can see light.*

Average Man: But do you know facts?

Strindberg: Facts? Study my *To Damascus.* You will find sublimated facts, the soul's battle with itself and the Devil. You will meet the Stranger, the Lady, the Beggar, the Doctor, the Sister, the Mother, the Old Man, the Confessor, the Abbess, the Fool, the Shadows, and the Children—yet they are all me, me having passed through sin and sorrow, through the uncleanliness and shame of life and who sees at last the white *Monastery on the Hill.* I have fathomed all humanity, suffered with all, been haunted by all, lived the awful mystery of existence.

Average Man (yawning): I don't want the awful mystery of existence. This sort of talk is rather boring. Have you nothing else?

Strindberg: My historical plays. Rows of them. With kings, queens, mistresses, ministers, priests, great movements, great faith, strong action, saints and sinners, wise men and fools. Read my *Master Olof, Sir Bengt's Wife, Eric the XIV, Gustavus Vasa, Charles the XII, Gustavus Adolphus, Christina.*

Average Man: It seems rather a lot and nothing that concerns me. All about Scandinavia. We want something new and more generally applicable.

Strindberg : There are my novels. There are my scientific writings, about astronomy, chemistry, physics, botany, geology, entomology, medicine, philology, political economy, alchemy, astrology, magnetism, hypnotism, spiritism, and Swedenborg. *There is my exposition of lunacy.*

Average Man: You are not wholesome. You're mad.

Strindberg: Yes; *mad* and *sane.*

Average Man: I give you up. I never met such a man.

Strindberg (his ghost dissolving): You will meet me again and again and again—in all humanity.

Average Man (settles down in his armchair to read *Punch*): *That will again be unpleasant.*

I am sure you will forgive the average man for "giving up." By this imaginary interview I have no wish to stigmatise any nation as being particularly incapable of understanding Strindberg. We all like to be able to pick up the figures of literature like marionettes and say—according to our ability to judge—Zola was a naturalist, Maeterlinck is a mystic, Nietzsche was an aristocrat, Tolstoy was a social reformer, etc. Strindberg was perhaps less understood in Sweden, the country of his birth, than in Germany or France. He evoked strong denunciation and lived for many years in bitter feud with Swedish literary tradition and judgment. Strindberg was not awarded the Nobel prize for literature. For 20 years he was attacked by the permanent Secretary of the Swedish Academy, the late Dr. C. D. af Wirsén. Wirsén wrote of Strindberg's "evil but empty wit," of his blasphemous effusions and ridiculous vanity. Wirsén received *The Father* with feelings of pity, for he could see nothing in it but the impotence of a diseased imagination and a mixture of coarseness and paradoxicality. *To Damascus* was to Wirsén a "horrid and depressing work—excessively loathsome." As Wirsén exercised considerable influence over the selection of recipients of the Nobel Prize in

Literature, which is awarded by the Swedish Academy, Strindberg did not receive favourable consideration.

I must concede at once that Strindberg was exceedingly troublesome to critics.

As a playwright he wrote naturalistic, historical, symbolical plays, dream plays, plays embodying strange shapes out of the subconscious, tender and innocent plays for little children, and plays which seemed to have been concocted in the kitchen of the devil.

As a novelist and writer of short stories he wrote in every style and without style. He wrote fine fresh living stories of the sea and of the fisherfolk, tales of tragedy and heroism, of the deepest spiritual problems of the human soul. He wrote also coarse and indecent tales, morbid, sexually embittered. He burst out in blasphemy and the desire for senseless destruction. He is the author of novels that can scarcely be called novels, for they are but thin disguises of bitter personal vendetta.

As social reformer he hit out right and left, above and below the belt, against convention, the State, the family, religion, marriage, women, universities and pompous learning. He attacked Dante, Shakespeare, Ibsen, and generally disparaged all the little gods of accepted excellence. His youthful attack on Dante reminds me of Herbert Spencer's comment on the pictures of the great and old masters.

As a student of Nature—manifest and occult—he poured out opinions on science, wild and extravagant ideas about the purpose of things. During a certain period of his life he applied himself mercilessly to the problem of making gold, experimenting with solutions of sulphate of iron. He dived into all the dark by-paths of the occult. Chemistry to him became alchemy, astronomy, astrology, physics, the servant of magic, and the form of man but the tool of mighty forces. He conversed with unseen powers and tried to capture wireless waves from the air. He became ridiculous in the eyes of scientific orthodoxy.

Add to these strange and redundant activities his authorship of novels, stories, autobiographies, dissertations, poems, essays, satirical sketches, books on dramaturgy, philology and the Chinese language.

Strindberg oscillated between self-elation, the sense of tremendous power, overtopping genius and self-contempt and pity for his own failures. Listen to his own description of his manner of writing (as described by Uddgren): "When I have finished my work for the day I always note on a piece of paper what I shall begin with the next day. The whole long afternoon and evening I collect material for the next day's work. During my morning walk my thoughts are further condensed, and when I return from my wanderings I am charged like an electric machine. I put on a dry vest, for after my walk I am always very hot, and then I sit down at my writing-table. As soon as I have paper and pen ready it bursts out. The words literally tumble over me, and the pen works under high pressure in order to get everything down on paper. When I have written for a while I have a feeling that I am floating in space. Then it is as if a higher will than my own made the pen glide over the paper, guide it to write down words which seem to me entirely inspired."

The same ecstasy of writing is shown in *Alone*, where he says of his life at the writing-table: "I live, and I live the manifold lives of all the human beings I describe, happy with those who are happy, evil with the evil ones, good with the good; I creep out of my own personality, and speak out of

the mouths of children, of women, of old men; I
am king and beggar, I have worldly power, I am
the tyrant and the most despised of all, the oppressed
hater of the tyrant; I hold all opinions and profess
all religions; I live in all times and have myself
ceased to be. This is a state which brings indescrib-
able happiness."

But sometimes the joy of literary creation gave
way to profound self-disgust. " What an occupation,"
he wrote in the *Quarantine Master's Tales,* " to sit
and flay one's fellow-humans, offer the skins for
sale, and expect people to buy them. It is like the
famished hunter who cuts off his dog's tail, eats the
meat himself, and gives the bones to the dog, the
dog's own bones. To go about spying out people's
secrets, exposing the birthmark of one's best friend,
using one's wife as a vivisection rabbit, storming like
a Croat, cutting down, violating, burning and selling.
The devil take it all."

Strindberg is as aggravating to the critic as was
Leonardo da Vinci, who was painter, sculptor, archi-
tect, poet, engineer, mathematician, philosopher.
Such minds make specialists who are capable of
doing only *one* thing very angry.

We are living in an age which is cursed by
specialists who can do one thing and one thing only,
and who consequently, having lost the powers of
comparison and the sense of relativity, do everything
badly.

Having considered the writer let us now give some
attention to the experiences of the man, to what he
was and tried to do before he became that composite
self of which we speak as August Strindberg. If it
be true that we make circumstances and have powers
of will and self-control, it is equally true that circumstances make us. Life is a constant response to

impression and experience. The outer circumstances
of Strindberg's life played a large part in moulding
the character of one who was abnormally sensitive
and impressionable. Let me first say that Strindberg
was throughout life the slave of a full mind and an
empty pocket. Sometimes very poor, he was nearly
always in the throes of economic insecurity.

Strindberg wrote the story of his life—not perhaps
without some decorations of phantasy—in his autobiographical novel in four volumes, entitled *The
Bondswoman's Son, Fermentation Time, In the Red
Room*, and *The Author*. These were written at the
age of 37. He tells us that he wrote the first volume
when he was tired, " saw no longer any object in life,
considered himself superfluous, thrown away." That
mood, I must say, did not last long. I said just now
that he wrote an autobiographical work in four
volumes. That is understating the extent of the
account he gave of himself. All his plays, all his
stories, are in a sense autobiographical, a record of
something felt and lived with intense emotion.

Strindberg was born in 1849. His father, whom
in disparagement of his parentage he often calls
" the grocer," was a merchant and shipping agent
who had married the daughter of a tailor who had
been a servant. She was the mother of his three
children. August was born a short time after the
union between the parents had been legalised. The
father cherished the ideals of the upper classes, the
mother remained essentially of the people. To
early impressions of the differences between father
and mother can be ascribed Strindberg's acute
consciousness of class. We should now call it an
" inferiority-complex." The family was poor and the
strictest economy was necessary. Strindberg tells us

(16)

that he recollects fear and hunger as his first sensations. He was afraid of darkness, of being beaten, of offending people, of falling down, of knocking against things, of being in the way, of the fists of his brothers, of father's and mother's chastisements.

It was not easy to avoid being in people's way, for the parents with seven children and two servants lived in three rooms. The furniture consisted mostly of cradles and beds; children slept on ironing boards and chairs. Baptisms and funerals alternated. The mother developed phthisis after the birth of her twelfth child.

As a little boy, August adored his mother, longed for her exclusive love, was jealous when she could not give him the attention and time he wanted. He was shy, proud, always self-conscious, always ready to see injustice where none was intended. Wanting to adore and, finding the adored object not perfect, he began to criticise. The mother became the object of analysis. He was torn between love for her and contempt for her faults. He says that a yearning for the mother followed him through life.

I cannot help adding a note of posthumous congratulation to Strindberg. It was a blessing for him that there was no Freud to analyse his " mother-complex."

When in later life Strindberg's attacks on women were criticised, he defended himself by declaring that he chid woman because he loved her so well.

August felt disgust with the daily drudgery of the household, with the eternal round of shopping, cooking, cleaning, and washing.

" Glorious moral institution," he cries; " holy family, inviolable, divine institution for the education of citizens in truth and virtue! Thou pretended home of virtues, where innocent children are tortured

B

to speak their first lie, where will-power is crushed
by despotism, where self-reliance is killed by narrow
egoism. Family, thou art the home of all social
vices, the charitable institution for all lazy women.
The forge for the chains of the breadwinner, and the
hell of the children! "

August did not shine at his first school, though
his knowledge was in advance of his years. He was
the youngest at school and at home, a position which
he resented. His was a school for the children of
the upper middle classes. He wore knickerbockers
of leather and strong coarse boots which smelt of
blubber and blacking. The boys in velvet blouses
avoided him. He observed that the badly dressed
boys were more severely beaten than the well-dressed
ones, and that nice-looking boys escaped altogether.

The early experiences of school were recorded
with characteristic vehemence : —

" . . . It was regarded as a preparation for hell and not for
life ; the teachers seemed to exist in order to torment, not to
punish. All life weighed like an oppressive nightmare, in which
it was of no avail to have known one's lessons when one left
home. Life was a place for punishing crimes committed before
one was born, and therefore the child walked about with a
permanently bad conscience."

At nine, he fell in love with the schoolmaster's
daughter, and at 15 he fell in love again, this time
with a woman of 30. All Strindberg's love affairs
had a roseate beginning and an end tinged with
tragedy.

That love of nature which ran through the stormy
life of Strindberg like a note of music was shown
early in life. The sea, the cliffs, the forest, the
green sward, gave him a peace of mind which
nothing else could impart. He loved the thousand
islands in the vicinity of Stockholm, the archipelago
which guards the fair capital of Sweden. He loved

the keen salt breezes, the white stems of the birches, and the evergreen storm-bound fir trees. Of this love he wrote, speaking of himself in the third person:

"This was his scenery, the true milieu of his nature, idylls, poor rugged rocks, covered with pine forest, thrown out on wide stormy fjords with the immense sea as a distant background. He remained true to this love . . . and neither the Alps of Switzerland, the olive-clad hills of the Mediterranean, nor the cliffs of Normandy could oust this rival."

Amongst all the disharmonies, sorrows, and temptations brought to the cradle of Strindberg by the Fates, there was one magic and precious gift. He was given the secret by which the nature mystic, when all social structure tumbles about his head, can enter into silent and blissful communion with the green life of earth.

The need to question authority, to dissect belief and tradition, was always insistent. When August and his brother were sent as boarders to spend a holiday in the house of a sexton, he saw the wafers being prepared and stamped for Holy Communion. He ate them and reflected that there was not much in the sacrament—a conclusion which later in life led him to express himself in a manner which brought him into court as defendant in an action for blasphemy. After all, questions and doubts about the nature of the sacramental bread have caused great and bitter schisms in the Christian Church, and are to-day prominent subjects of anxious discussion amongst steady bishops of the Established Church.

Strindberg oscillated, early and ever afterwards, between self-confidence and self-reproach; if he tormented others he also tormented himself.

When his mother lay dying the thought of a little ring, which she had promised him after her death, crossed his mind. He battled with the shameful

(19)

thought, and years afterwards he could remember the pangs of remorse which pursued him.

The thirst for knowledge, knowledge of every kind and at all costs, was another key-note of his life. Every subject interested him, until he had mastered it. He wanted to know everything, to be able to do everything. As a child his desire to know was tinged with jealousy of the achievements of others. His brother had been praised for his drawing. August wanted to draw. His brothers and sisters could all play some instrument. August wanted to play, but without practising scales. He taught himself to play the piano and learned to read and copy music.

A stepmother had taken the place of his mother in the home. She professed great religious devotion and oppressed August excessively. He wanted to out-do her in religious exercises and imposed severe restrictions upon himself, shunned worldly pleasures for a time and studied Thomas à Kempis. Whilst the stepmother broke the Sabbath, August kept it rigorously, and felt sure that God would take due notice.

As a man he thought he knew better than others —we may accede he often did. When well advanced in life he wrote the following to Count Birger Mörner : —

"Through discontent with yourself you ennoble yourself. Be therefore discontented at times and feel despair. That breaks up the blocks of stone which conceal the ore. Pass through seven burning hells and come out on the other side unsinged. *O crux ave spes unica.*"

The education of Strindberg was not neglected. It has sometimes been said that he was " self-taught " in the ordinary sense of that expression. He had

every opportunity to absorb the subjects taught in
the public schools which he attended—Greek, Latin,
modern languages, history and science. But he was
certainly self-taught in the wider sense of this term.
One Latin master called him an idiot and was
probably quite genuine in his conviction. Many a
genius has been dubbed an idiot.

Having felt thoroughly religious he had, perforce,
to become a free thinker. The puritanical phase
was brought to an end through acquaintance with
literature. The schoolboy began to read Shakespeare,
Dickens, Walter Scott, Alexandre Dumas. Literature,
as a great tradition and interpretation of human
problems, became known to him. The belletristic and
puritanical conceptions of life presented themselves
in their most profound antithesis. His range of
reading became wide and varied, as were the demands
of his many-sided self.

But as he felt himself master of both religion
and free thought, he could not resist an invitation to
preach during the summer holidays, when he was
tutor in a country vicarage. The practice of per-
mitting serious-minded students and undergraduates
to try their priestly powers was not uncommon. The
idea proved glorious and irresistible to August. The
local big-wigs—the Baron, the Baroness, the Squire
and the Ladies would all have to sit and listen
reverently to August, as the mouthpiece of the Lord.
The obstacle of being a free thinker had to be overcome, and was overcome after a little accommodating
talk with the Vicar. The Church was filled with
people when August climbed to the pulpit, in
clerical garb and with beating heart. He spoke on
conversion through free will and opened the gates
of heaven to all, publicans and sinners, rulers and
harlots—and denounced his old friends who were

sunk in cruel and hypocritical self-conceit. ' He was deeply moved by his own eloquence.

The success of the sermon confirmed August's contempt of orthodox religion. He became the ringleader of a section of youths in the highest class in the *gymnasium* who, in spite of threats and reprimands, refused to attend morning prayers. When his father begged him to go to Church, August replied: "Preach, I can do that myself."

In May, 1867, August passed his matriculation (*Studentexamen*) and the gates of the university were open to him. Between 1867 and 1872 Strindberg spent periods at the university of Upsala, trying to achieve success as a dutiful learner, submissive to the discipline of professorial authority.

Poverty pursued him. Breakfast and supper consisted of a glass of milk and a bun. He was not a promising student. Attendance at lectures served chiefly as a stimulus to his critical faculties. He found the methods of teaching literature and philosophy tedious and ineffective, the professors ignorant and plebeian. At the end of the first term, being without money, he returned to Stockholm in search of remunerative work. He found a situation as teacher in a Stockholm Board School at a yearly salary of £50; this seemed to him opulence. He observed the effects of poverty on the children of the poor.

"Suffering," he writes, " has stamped on the faces of the lower classes that expression of hopelessness and torment which neither religious resignation nor the hope of heaven can obliterate, and from which the upper classes flee as from an evil conscience."

He studied the penalty of industrialism, and observed that the children of the manual labourer looked more sickly and less intelligent than those of the upper class:

" The trade-diseases of the urban working-man seemed to be transmitted; here one saw in miniature the lungs and the blood of the gas-worker, ruined through sulphurous fumes; the shoulders and flattened feet of the smith; the brain of the painter atrophied through the fumes of varnish and poisonous paints; the scrofulous eruption of the sweep; the contracted chest of the bookbinder; here one heard the echo of the cough of the metal-worker and the asphalt manufacturer, smelt the poisons of the wall-paper maker; noticed the watchmaker's myopia in new editions."

His sympathy with the working classes was no passing sentiment. The insistent plea for social justice is clearly heard through the jumble of some of his later outbursts against the social order. Rebellious contempt of current morals and respectability rose as a mighty force in the mind of this extraordinary schoolmaster.

He did not live virtuously. His sense-life was awake and he recognised no necessity for restraint. The strivings after ascetic peace which had filled his adolescence had now been laid aside ; with the breaking of his faith in the watchful solicitude of Jesus, natural impulses had been set free. His autobiography records his early struggles and his later fall with the same detached imperturbability. He lacks the sense of shame which avoids certain topics. He observes no reticences. The pages in many of his books are studded with coarse language and unsavoury references to physical life. The sexual cynicism which pervades the story of his life is only relieved by his perfect sincerity.

He describes the pleasures of inebriation with similar frankness. At the age of 19 he was already familiar with Bacchic revels. His brain was inflamed with ideas, congested with unformulated thought. The narcosis of alcohol attracted him.

Strindberg later on explained the craving for alcohol by the lack of nourishing diet in Upsala and the dullness of his home in Stockholm. He wrote of himself: "Like the rest of the race, he was born of drunkards, generation after generation, from pagan times immemorial, when ale and mead were used, and the desire had inevitably become a necessity."

Strindberg was not a success as a board school teacher. He was restless. He read Byron and Schiller, and longed for escape.

Life obligingly offered him a new part in which to act. He became a student of Medicine. A friend, an old doctor, invited Strindberg to stay in his home, where he could combine the duty of tutor to the sons of the doctor with the study of Medicine. The idea was attractive. For in spite of the dreary prospect of eight years' medical studies, the profession of Medicine seemed the portal to enviable knowledge. "To become a sage who understood life's riddles" —that was his dream for the moment. He thought that the life of a physician would be that of freedom encompassed by real wisdom, penetrating mysteries.

The experiences of his medical education soon became distasteful. The old physician took his pupil to see patients rich and poor, providing him with diverse clinical material. He was asked to assist at early morning operations and to hold the patients. Whilst Strindberg held the patient's head, the doctor "removed glands with a fork." The assistant's thoughts were soaring high above the surgery, in the regions of Goethe's *Faust* and Wieland's novels;

they were with Georges Sand, Chateaubriand and Lessing. During cauterisation the smell of human flesh rose in his nostrils and spoilt his appetite for breakfast. He describes his state of mind in the following words: " Imagination had been set in motion and memory would not work; reality with its burns and blood clots was ugly ; æstheticism had seized the youth, and life seemed dull and repulsive." Failure at the preliminary medical examination at Upsala precipitated his decision not to enter a profession which was exclusively occupied with the aches of the body.

Meanwhile in the evenings he saw the glories of the stage from a seat in the gallery. He announced his intention of becoming an actor. For some months he lived in an ideal stage world. He studied Schiller's lecture " On the Theatre as an Institution for Moral Education," and saturated his mind with a lofty and idealistic conception of the ethical and æsthetic mission of the stage. Was not this the greatest of all human arts ? He buried his past restlessness in the search for knowledge of the actor's gifts and graces. He studied the pose of antique sculpture and practised to walk with uplifted head and expanded chest. He tried to conquer his shyness and his fear of crossing open places. His vocal and dramatic exercises were undertaken with such zest that they disturbed the peace of the doctor's house, in which he still lived, and had to be continued out-of-doors. He stormed, he tells us, against heaven and earth.

But the prosaic training at the school of dramatic art followed, and there was the usual conflict between dream and reality. Strindberg's wish to make his *début* in an important part was rudely brushed aside. After some humiliating experiences, he was given

a small part in Björnson's *Mary Stuart*. He appeared
as a nobleman, and all his dramatic energy was
perforce encompassed in the following sentence:
" The Peers have sent an emissary with a challenge
to the Earl of Bothwell." It was bitterly insigni-
ficant, but it seemed a portal to greater achievement.

Something happened at this performance which
should be noted. Siri von Essen, then Baroness
Wrangel, who was later on to become his wife, was
present, and saw Strindberg for the first time.
Neither of them knew of the momentous meeting.

The usual processes of disillusionment were soon
at work. The boards and the paint, which when seen
from the gallery had held so much charm, were
now dusty and ugly. The actors who were permitted
to play great parts were, after all, just like ordinary
mortals. They yawned loudly between their turns
and gave expression to commonplace sentiments as
a relief from the sublimities uttered on the stage.
After some months, during which Strindberg was
only a super, he was heartily tired of the whole
thing. He felt repressed and misjudged. He
demanded his right to be tried and judged. He
was given an important part and a special rehearsal
at which he appeared without stage costume and
without the requisite enthusiasm. He shouted his
sentences in a manner which made it clear that he
was in need of further instruction. He was advised
to resume his pupilage. But this he would not do.
The humiliation was unbearable. He cried with
rage and decided to commit suicide. An opium pill,
which he had treasured with a view to the possibility
of having to summon a catastrophic end to life's
difficulties, was utilised for the purpose, but failed
altogether of a calamitous effect.

AUGUST STRINDBERG

A friend who knew the better way re-awakened Strindberg's interest in earthly existence through a merry drinking bout. Out of the misery that followed, his creative faculties rose insistent. He wrote his first play, a comedy in two acts, and it was written in four days. He tells us that he felt as if years of pain were over, as if an abscess had been lanced. He was so happy that something sang within him. When his first effort in drama had been submitted to the criticism of the friends who assembled in his garret, and they had saluted him as an author, August fell on his knees and thanked God, Who had delivered him out of his difficulties and given him the gift of literary expression.

A feverish period of production followed. In two months he wrote two comedies, a tragic verse drama and some poems. But the first comedy which had been submitted to the manager of the Royal Theatre was not accepted; the tragedy, which he had also sent in, met with the same fate. Strindberg's last appearance on the stage was ignominious, yet symbolic of his future as a writer of drama. No part whatever had been found for him. He offered to act as prompter and was accepted.

Returning to Upsala, he was determined to distinguish himself by obtaining his degree or by writing a successful play. Poverty could not be shaken off. His room was squalid. The rain came through the ceiling, firewood was scarce, and occasional frugal suppers of bread and water were forcible reminders of life's realities. He managed, nevertheless, to study æsthetics and living languages with a new ardour.

Ibsen and Björnson dominated the intellectual horizon in Scandinavia at the time. Strindberg had been deeply stirred by *Brand*. But Ibsen's *Nora* roused the instinctive sex-antagonism in Strindberg. He hated *Nora*, and his lust for opposition to matriarchal ideas became predominant. It is not difficult to trace this antagonism to Ibsen in Strindberg's later writings against women.

His struggle to become a dramatist continued. He wrote a one-act play entitled *In Rome* in a fortnight. The play dealt with the Danish sculptor Thorvaldsen's first stay in Rome. The play was accepted and performed in the autumn of 1870 at the Royal Theatre in Stockholm. The author was 21 years old. He watched the play standing in his old place in the gallery, feeling acute pangs of self-criticism. He felt as if he had been under an electric battery. His legs trembled and he wept with nervousness.

" Every stupidity," Strindberg writes, " which had slipped into the verse shook him and jarred upon his ears." He saw nothing but imperfections in his work. His ears burned with shame, and he ran out before the curtain fell. Drowning in the rapid waters of Norrström now seemed the only atonement. The incident is characteristic of the man. The thoughts which · a few months before had seemed to be a perfect expression of his imagination were now outside their author, dismissed, objects of pity. He had grown whilst the imperfect words lay dead on the paper. The sorrows of the evening were drowned in carousals, in food and drink and other gratification of the lower man.

During this time in Upsala there was much heavy drinking, much discussion of worthy philosophies, and much storming against the accepted and settled order of things by the young men who formed Strindberg's coterie. He decided to pass his examination in Latin composition. He had not made the requisite preparation, called upon the Professor in a state of after-dinner exaltation, demonstrated his independence of spirit, and was promptly turned out. This humiliation, coupled with the tragedy of the suicide of a student, which unnerved him, again brought to his mind the thought of putting an end to life. A friend found Strindberg with a bottle of prussic acid and sinister intentions, which were happily averted in the usual alcoholic manner. Strindberg had written a tragedy in five acts, called *Blotsven*, depicting the struggle between the spirit of the Viking and proselytising Christianity. Convinced of its unworthiness, he had burnt the MS. He re-wrote it under the title of *The Outlaw* and sent it to the theatre.

With three of his friends he spent a summer in a fisherman's cottage on one of the Baltic Islands outside Stockholm, and threw himself into a healthy outdoor life, bathing, sailing, fencing. The body was to be taught natural goodness and the counsels of Satan were to be unheeded. He studied philology, avoided alcohol, and dwelt with Dante, Shakespeare and Goethe, as he had shortly before dwelt with Kierkegaard, Oehlenschläger, Kant and Schopenhauer.

Returning to Upsala, he was again tormented by poverty, and had to borrow from his friends. His room had a bed without sheets or pillow cases. Kind friends were responsible for an irregular supply of food. There was a stove pipe in the room, which was hot every Thursday, when the landlady did her washing. Then he stood reading, with his hands behind his back, leaning against the pipe, with a chest of drawers doing service as a real desk. His viking play had meanwhile been accepted. The first performance was received coldly. The critics were ungracious; he was accused of having borrowed the form from Ibsen, though the cold, restrained and rugged simplicity of the language was directly inspired by the Icelandish Sagas.

Sick at heart, Strindberg resumed his battle with poverty and dejection. The darkness of uncertainty was again upon him, when, with the suddenness which is usually reserved for good boys in fairy tales, Fortuna held out her hand.

He received a letter announcing that the King was interested in his play and wished to see him. He could not believe his eyes and suspected that the letter was a joke. On being reassured of the genuineness of the message, he went to Stockholm, and was received by His Majesty King Charles XV. The King smiled as the young author made his way to the Royal presence through lines of courtiers and greeted him with geniality. Charles XV, himself a poet, expressed the pleasure which he had derived from the viking play and his personal interest in the revival of the old Norse Tales. After enquiries regarding Strindberg's financial prospects, the King ordered a yearly stipend of 800 kronor to be paid to him from the privy purse. Strindberg left the palace moved and grateful, with the first quarterly instalment of the monarch's bounty in his pocket.

This early play foreshadowed Strindberg's mastery of the art of drama, showed that he possessed that power of visualising and speaking through the characters of a play with equally apportioned interest which is essential to the true dramatist.

For a time the royal stipend made a great difference. He enjoyed a sense of freedom from the pressure of poverty, the achievement of some measure of success expanded his chest and straightened his back. He struggled through his examination in philology, astronomy and sociology. He read the history of philosophy, but his brain was filled with creative energy and the path of learning was blocked. One evening he evoked the anger of one of the Professors by attacking Dante. Dante was ignorant of Greek and therefore uncultured. He was not a philosopher, as he suppressed thought by revelation. He was a foolish monk, who sent unbaptised children to hell. Dante had shown bad taste, for amongst the greatest poets of the world he had placed Homer, Horace, Lucanus, Ovid, Virgil—and himself. The result of this observation was that Strindberg was denounced as insolent and crazy.

A period of increased mental distress and uncertainty followed. He took to painting. This was something that would condense and support the evaporating ego. To paint a green landscape in the midst of dull winter and to hang it on one's wall —that was something worth doing! He locked himself in with easel, brushes and paint and gave himself up to colour-worship.

His friends, excluded, discussed him on the other side of the door. They talked as if they were speaking of somebody who was ill. "Now he is painting, too!" said one of the friends in a tone of deep depression. Strindberg heard and came to the conclusion that he was going mad. Fearing compulsory incarceration, he wrote to the manager of a private asylum in which the patients were allowed their liberty and to till the soil. He expressed his willingness to submit to the curative principles of the institution. The reply was kind and reassuring. The manager had made enquiries about the would-be patient and found that there was no need for extreme steps.

Three months passed and a second instalment of the royal stipend was not paid. A letter of humble enquiry brought the reply that His Majesty had never intended to give permanent support to Strindberg and that it was only intended as a temporary help. A further sum was enclosed, as His Majesty had decided to help his *protégé* once more. Ten years later Strindberg heard that he had been wrongfully accused of writing defamatory verse about the King.

The time came to leave Upsala. The page of life was turned, and on the next was written journalism. At a valedictory gathering of the old friends he thanked them for their contributions to his self— "For a personality is not developed out of itself: out of each soul with which it comes in contact it sucks a drop like the bee collecting its honey from millions of flowers, transforming it and passing it on as its own."

Behold him now filling an ill-paid post on a Stockholm radical paper. He plunged into art criticism, passed through a brief but eventful attachment to a ladies' illustrated paper, again tried to become an actor, found employment as an editor on a new paper published in the interests of the insurance system, failed, fell into despair, fled to the sea, lived for some time at Sandhamn amongst pilots and coastguardsmen.

Taunted with failing in everything, Strindberg aspired to a clerkship in a local telegraph office and diligently practised the art of the telegraph operator. After a month, he was allowed to send off weather telegrams. (I am sure these were usually portents of storm.) Two shipwrecks off the coast supplied material for picturesque and vivid description, which he made use of in a Stockholm paper. This led to another venture in journalism and all seemed smooth for a time. But he soon learned that one must not

aim at too wide a view-point or express oneself too
freely. The ideal and the real newspapers are two
very different things. To write in strict conformity
with party colour and convention—was a rule which
Strindberg could not follow. He reported the debates
in the Riksdag in such a disrespectful manner that
a less critical man had to take his place. He reviewed
a Christian journal by declaring that the journalist
had incurred a heavy responsibility by spreading such
errors. When allowed to act as dramatic critic of
the performances at the Royal Theatre he took the
opportunity of paying off old scores. There were
many complaints against him, and he was even
threatened with a thrashing by a theatrical company
which was smarting under his attacks. It was evident
that his services were not appreciated, and Strindberg
relieved the newspaper of his embarrassing presence.

The University with its rigid forms of instruction
and its standards of learning had been like a cage
on the bars of which he had exercised his muscles
of independence. He had craved for freedom and
yet the milieu in which he now found himself did
not bring the satisfaction anticipated. The journalists
with whom he mingled lacked the culture which
the University imposes. They talked in ready-made
phrases and on subjects over which they had no
mental mastery. They mistook the gossip of the
news-hunter for judicial wisdom. Strindberg chose
his friends among the artists. They were shabbily
dressed, cultivated vile manners, were gloriously
illiterate, but they had originality of feeling and
thought. Strindberg still found solace of mind
in painting. But his mind was in a state of
perpetual ferment. He felt irritated with all that
was old and antiquated. A philosophic friend
comforted and calmed him by la Bruyère's saying:

" Do not distress yourself over the stupidity and wickedness of human beings; you may just as well distress yourself over the fallen stone : both are subservient to the same laws : to be stupid and to fall."

"Yes, it is all very well to say that. But to be a bird and compelled to live in a mine! Air, light, I cannot breathe ; nor see ! " he burst out. "I am dying of suffocation ! "

" Write," said his friend.

" Yes, but what ? "

Out of the mists of doubt, the volatility of convictions, there rose creatures clad in flesh and blood, the warring selves of his multiple personality. The thin silhouettes of history became instinct with life, and Strindberg's first great drama, *The Heretic*, afterwards named *Master Olof*, was conceived.

He wrote it during two summer months of quiet life on his island in the Baltic. *Master Olof* deals with the Swedish Protestant Reformation. In the personality of Olaus Petri, the Swedish Luther, Strindberg had found all the elements needed for an historical drama of the soul's battles and final defeat by the world. The conflict of personality in this drama makes it rich in contrasts, but they are softened by an atmosphere of fatalistic resignation before the irreconcilability of ideas. When he heard that the play had been rejected, the bitterness of failure worked havoc in his soul. He threw himself into the study of social problems and found human follies supreme in principles of Government and in the judgment of majorities and minorities. He took on a new rôle, that of sceptic, materialist, atheist, and strove to free himself from prejudice, social, religious and moral. " He had but one opinion, that everything was wrong; but one conviction, that nothing could be done to make things better at present, but one hope, that some day the time for interference would come and that things would then improve."

Strindberg was one of a coterie of artists, writers and dilettanti, who assembled in the evenings in the Red Room of Berns Restaurant. The tone was free, the clamour for truth loud and contemptuous of the treasures of the past. The company was held together by an aggressive scepticism which was wholly sincere. The axiom that the spring of human action is egoism was the basis of argument and hypocrisy was hunted down with relentless severity. The old was to be destroyed and the new created.

A period of bitter want, illness and humiliation followed; depression and dislike of human society overtook him. Sometimes he wished that death or lunacy would set him free.

At this time, there occurred one of those sudden changes of circumstances which entered often in the sombre warp and woof of Strindberg's destiny, like a thread of scarlet. Following a friend's advice, he had applied for the post of Assistant Librarian in the Royal Library of Stockholm. His application was successful, and in 1874 he again placed his foot on the step-ladder of social respectability, redeemed by the title of Royal Secretary. He was able to throw himself into the depths of human thought contained in the vast number of books, of which he was now master, with the eagerness of one who is so thirsty that he wants to drink the sea. New passion, new disillusionment, for he found that the great problems of life, those that last through centuries and chaff the impotence of the human mind, remain problems. He felt the need of undertaking a solid and circumscribed piece of work. He undertook to catalogue Chinese MSS., and devoted a year to the study of the Chinese language. He

(35)

wrote a Memoir, which was read at the Académie des Inscriptions et Belles Lettres. Correspondence with sinologues all over the world followed, together with membership of learned societies and a medal from the Imperial Russian Geographical Society.

Strindberg tells us that at this period of his life he had succeeded in contracting a healthy idiotism.

Strindberg's relations to women and his three unhappy marriages were the fountain of soul-racking experience from which he emerged, possibly not wiser, but certainly more powerful as an interpreter of himself and of humanity. The women he loved were injured by him, inasmuch as he made their real and imagined failings the subject of brutal biographical romance. The fact that the blame fell upon him, not upon the victims of his conjugal experimentation, would scarcely compensate for the painful publicity with which he punished the women and unburdened himself.

Worthy people have agitated themselves over the question whether Strindberg was a real evil-liver or not. He was certainly an evil-liver in the sense of conventional morality. In giving free play to the impulses of his ever-expanding personality, he played the colossal egotist and sinned against the laws of God and man. If by evil-liver we understand a craven sensualist or a man beset with Don Juanesque frivolities, he was not one.

There was nothing of the light-hearted immoralist of the comic stage, or the poetic profligacy of Robert Burns, about Strindberg; he acted throughout the heavy tragedian in the inexorable drama of sex-antagonism.

The Confession of a Fool, which Strindberg himself called " a terrible book," is a nauseating record of his first marriage, in which love and lust, hatred and disgust, adoration and contempt, exultation and misery, are set forth in their psychological relation to a sexual love, the disappointment of which lashed the artist in Strindberg into fury against woman. The ghost of Strindberg's first wife never left his side. In the *Confession* she is portrayed as a beautiful siren with golden hair, adorably small feet and a false heart—a fiend in female form, with the soul of a prostitute and the worst vices of a loathsome debauchee. She reappears in his dramas *The Father, Comrades, The Link*; in his stories and essays; in different characters, drawn with a pen dipped in gall, retouched and seen in different perspective, but always the cause of man's degradation or downfall.

There are two sides to every marriage. In the case of Strindberg's first marriage, the other side has now been told, for his eldest daughter, Karin Smirnoff, has written a book entitled *Strindberg's First Wife*, which is not only a loving and generous attempt to clear her mother's memory, but a just and deeply moving account of the conflict of two souls. If one could take the two books and dissolve them together, the rising mists of love and anguish, disillusionment, hate, clashing wills and final reconciliation—though not on the physical plane—would take the shape of Charity.

Siri von Essen, of a distinguished family, was the wife of Baron Carl Gustaf Wrangel, of the Life Guards, when Strindberg first met her. He fell desperately in love, and she fought hard against an attraction which threatened to engulf her. In March, 1876, he wrote to her:—

"I want, I want to be mad ! Now I have told everything. To whom? To the spring, to the sun,

to the oaks, to the willow-blossoms, to the anemones,
and the bells sang it and the lark said ' do it.'
What have I told ?—That I love you ! ! ! ! And
I walk the streets as proud as a king, and I look
compassionately on the mob. Why don't you fall
down on your dirty faces before me ? Do you not
know that She loves me ? Who ? The princess,
my princess, the most beautiful woman in Sweden,
she who has the bluest eyes, the smallest feet, the
most golden hair, the most beautiful brow, the most
delicate hands.—You are not worthy to hear it ! ! ! !
She with the greatest heart, the proudest mind, the
noblest feelings, the most beautiful thoughts ! Mine,
my beloved—and she loves me, wretch that I am.
—If she does not soon desert me, I shall go mad
with conceit."

And a few days later she wrote : —
" There is then still on earth love that rises above
all other—so free from sensual impressions, so holy
and pure.—Oh! my most beautiful, my sweetest
dream, has it thus become real ! What am I,
unworthy creature, that God grants me such
happiness ? . . . This love . . . this innermost union
of souls—it is a breath from Heaven, it is the
feeling one wishes to give to one's God."*

She had always wanted to be an actress, but the
realisation of that wish was impossible under the
rigidly conventional conditions of her marriage.
He besought her to free herself from the shackles
of an unreal marriage (her husband had fallen in
love with a young cousin), and to join him. He
wanted her as his wife. He wanted to help her to
develop her gifts, to become a great actress. He
wrote wild and passionate letters : —" If you have
not the courage to live without me, if you have not

Strindberg's Första Hustru.

the courage to live with me—then die with me and
let our love continue on the other side of death,
pure and holy, when we shall be free from these
miserable bodies which drag down everything ! Die
with me—Oh ! in your company I should joyfully
pass into the infinite unknown spheres, where our
souls may embrace one another without having
to be ashamed, or ask leave of anyone but God.
Now, forgive me all this, you must, you must, for
I love you ! "

What love-letters from the hater of woman, what
soaring flights on the wings of dreams !

" Thirty years afterwards," writes the daughter of
August Strindberg and Siri von Essen, " Siri testified
that she had loved him with a limitless love."

A divorce, by mutual agreement, was arranged
and Strindberg and Siri were married in December,
1877.   A child was prematurely born, a weakly
infant who died soon afterwards.   There were three
other children of this marriage, Karin, Greta and
Hans.   During the first years there was complete
agreement between the two in regard to the rights
of women.   Strindberg promised to be a champion
of women's rights.   " I shall be your spokesman,"
he said.   Those were happy years.   The *Confession
of a Fool* represents a mood, a phase, a temper,
but does not contain the full story of the marriage.
The hate and loathing which fill its pages were as
real as the adoration of the first love-letters.   For
Strindberg was woman-worshipper and woman-hater.
By the side of the man of passion to whom a woman
was a necessity, there was in him the monk who
feared and detested the coils of the sensual life.
The indecencies which he uttered came out of the
depths of self-detestation.   The woman-worshipper
fell in love—the woman-hater looked on the fall

with a sneer, cursed the bondage of ten years of married hell and finally related, in the public confessional, in sibilant tones of revenge, the intimate details of the conjugal struggle.

During the first years of marriage Strindberg emerged as a forcible writer, a personality compelling attention. He wrote a number of books—books which could not possibly be ignored, even by the most complacent community.

In 1877 a collection of short stories appeared entitled *From Fjärdingen and Svartbäcken*, which described the undergraduates' life at Upsala and caused annoyance in its exposure of the swamps and pitfalls in the academical training ground. They exposed traditional cant, humbug and lies.

He published a novel called *The Red Room*, which produced an outburst of anger and admiration. Voltaire's words, "*Rien n'est si désagréable que d'être pendu obscurément,*" had been chosen by Strindberg as a motto for the book and in protest against the treatment he had received. The force and style of *The Red Room* effectively protected its author from continued obscurity. Strindberg's name was made by this book; henceforth it was the war-cry of opposing factions.

Everything that is dishonest, cruel, banal, hypocritical and vile in the social system is exposed to view in the pages of *The Red Room*, which still, after fifty years, retain their freshness and the warmth of the burning moral indignation which caused them to be written.

He had found in the depth of the human heart the seven deadly sins, and he traced their poison in every human relationship, under the cloak of respectability, in the qualities which lead to worldly success and honour. Oblique finance, dishonest company-promoting, show philanthropy, unctuous religiosity, servile journalism, create characters which are drawn in bold and dark outline with strongly concentrated colours, but without the exaggeration of which he was accused. The characters are so typical of human weakness and wickedness, the psychological analysis of motives and acts so accurate, that the indictment of the book remains true in spite of changes in social form and personal types. The pompous publisher who grows fat on the brains of young authors, whilst he intimidates them by depreciation; the editor who finds favour with his party and his employers by suppressing every unwelcome truth and spreading every useful party lie; the moneylender who builds up a banking business through exploitation of the financial ruin of others are contrasted with the unsuccessful and the unworldly.

The publication of *The Red Room* was followed by an intense literary activity on the part of its restless author. He had found his tongue, and he had found an audience.

The versatility of mind and production which was the despair of his critics became apparent. *The Secret of the Guild*, a comedy in four acts, was published in 1880.

This play reflects a middle-age atmosphere and harmonises with Strindberg's earlier plays in its vivid presentation of the struggle between two generations. *Master Olof*, revised by Strindberg five times, was performed at the Swedish Theatre in 1880 and was a great success. It was no longer possible to forget him as a dramatist.

The Journey of Lucky Peter satirises humanity and Society in its narrative of what befell Peter, who wanted to see the world and taste its luxuries, but

like all good fairy-tales the drama ends happily, and
Peter regains peace of heart, and finds his dual-soul.
And the satire is tempered with a humour so
sympathetic, an understanding of the doers and
victims of evil so delicate, that the reader of this
fairy play puts down the book with a sigh of satisfaction that, after all, the worst experiences in this
world prove themselves to be but necessary milestones
of the pilgrim's progress. Lucky Peter, who discovers
the nothingness of the rich man's pleasures, of the
king's power, the bitterness of fame, the change-
ability of human institutions! We envy him his
rapid liberation from the chains of flesh, the severe
tuition under his fairy-teacher. The charm of the
play is irresistible; it has the mysterious eventfulness of
Peter Pan and *The Blue Bird*, but none of the fatui-
ties which often distort plays for children of all ages.

Sir Bengt's Wife was published in 1882. During
1880-82 a work, entitled *Old Stockholm*, appeared
with Strindberg and Claes Lundin as joint authors.
In this book Strindberg wrote on guilds and orders,
legends and superstitions, street music and amuse-
ments, slang, fauna and flora of the city of his birth.
This was followed by a popular history of Swedish
culture called *The Swedish People*. This caused
angry criticism and resentment of the sceptical
manner in which time-worn and honoured tenets
were treated. Strindberg gathered his forces for a
fresh attack on Society.

The New Kingdom also appeared in 1882 and
contained a series of satirical descriptions of the ideals
and conduct of the inhabitants of the "new kingdom"
which was supposed to have been created by the
Swedish constitution of 1865. The book is an attack
upon everything that average humanity holds dear ;
the scorching satire plays like lightning upon

royalty, militarism, history, aristocracy, bureaucracy, the press, the theatre, and, with special annihilative pleasure, on the Swedish Academy. It was impossible to deny that Strindberg had descended from generalisations to portraiture, that well-known and highly respected personages had been pilloried and caricatured. Affronted Society declared the book to be simply a lampoon on spotless individuals. Though the personal attacks were doubtless in bad form, and, though there are passages in the book which strain ridicule to the point of the grotesque and the vulgar, the brilliant wit, the profusion of ideas, and, above all, the incomparably good temper place *The New Kingdom* in the forefront of contemporary satirical writings. An affinity with Max Nordau is noticeable in certain chapters.

The year which saw the storm of *The New Kingdom* also witnessed more moderate winds in the first instalment of *Swedish Destinies and Adventures*, a collection of stories in historical setting which showed Strindberg as an interpreter of the genial and peaceful aspects of life, as a humorous onlooker, whose memory is stored with pictures of the kaleidoscopic reign of joy and sorrow, sin and virtue. Now and then the fresh narrative is oppressed by a distant rumble of the preacher who finds it difficult to suppress his views on women, political economy and over-rated civilisation.

Swedish Destinies and Adventures had reconciled the critics to Strindberg's existence. There was talent—undoubtedly; there was a mine of creative imagination; there was a calm current of lyrical content which the wild torrents of satire and abuse had not swallowed. Perhaps he might yet be redeemed, tamed to run a less dangerous and offensive literary course?

AUGUST STRINDBERG

Poems in Verse and Prose appeared in 1883. His poems were a challenge to the phrase-mongers and purists in hot and rugged verse, which acted like an over-dose of pepper on the jaded literary palate. There were lapses of metre and faults of rhyme, which the author defiantly stated were deliberate sacrifices of form to thought. The poet intoduced him work by a militant preface, in which he declared he was a challenger who was forced to employ the weapons chosen by his opponents.

Let us cast a glance at Strindberg during these years of intense literary activity before he left Sweden. He was not only a challenger of the order social, not only a weaver of thoughts and a spinner of words. He could be jovial and kind and humorous. He encouraged his wife to write, and even admired what she wrote. Together they produced an illustrated book for children. He could be full of fun and merry as a boy. The first years, before the publication of *The New Kingdom,* were really happy. They respected each other as artists. They entertained and were entertained at jolly gatherings of literary and artistic friends. Strindberg was so inordinately proud of his little daughter Karin, that when visitors came he insisted on awaking the baby late in the evening to show her to his friends, and when she, dazed from sleep and blinking in the bright light, burst into a baby's radiant smile he noted with enthusiasm how remarkably intelligent she was!

Those who have seen Mr. Robert Loraine in *The Father* will be interested in Strindberg's own description of his paternal feelings during the time which precedes the birth of Karin: "The wife who hitherto had been a comrade was endowed with another value as mother, and the ugly side of their relationship, which already had been noticeable, disappeared. A great, high mutual interest ennobled the relationship, made it more intimate and roused dormant forces to activity. This time of waiting was more beautiful than the period of the engagement and the honeymoon, and the arrival of the child the most beautiful in his life."

Siri was now engaged at the Royal Theatre, gaining considerable recognition as an actress of promise and talent. But the arduous experiences of child-birth and motherhood stood in the way of complete devotion to a career. During the summers the family lived on one of Strindberg's beloved islands. Siri managed the little home, Strindberg found time for gardening and taking his children on expeditions to pick flowers. Literary success had brought some affluence to the family. Strindberg was always improvident ; money came and disappeared too quickly. Economic anxieties played no small part in fomenting marital dissonances.

Sweden became too hot—or too cold, it is difficult to say which—for Strindberg. He wanted to leave. The wider intellectual life of the European Continent attracted him. The family left Sweden in 1883 and did not return for six years. When they returned the love and the happiness of the two, who had joined their fates in such jubilant expectation, were in ruins.

Siri, who was torn from friends and whose career as an actress was ended, disliked leaving Sweden. Strindberg's irritability, suspiciousness and nervous instability had greatly increased. They lived in many places, in Grez, Paris, Lausanne, Pegli, Genoa, Geneva, Weggis, Gersau, Izzigazbühl, Copenhagen, etc.

In Paris Strindberg met other Scandinavian writers of distinction, Björnson and Lie. A friendship sprang up between Strindberg and Björnson which was rich in sympathy and exchange of ideas. In *The Author* Strindberg gives us his impressions of Björnson, and Björnson has written an interesting description of Strindberg. Strindberg found Björnson a complex of personalities, consisting of the preacher, the peasant, the theatrical manager and the good child. Björnson found Strindberg young throughout, at home everywhere, free everywhere, an incurable idealist in whose eyes something sinister battled with something roguish.

By the side of the massive Norwegian, Strindberg at first experienced an unusual sense of security.

Björnson's democratic drama *The King* had been attacked as *lèse-majesté* and a political scandal. They had many experiences in common, were relatives in thought. Björnson in exile appealed to whatever vestige of hero-worship was left in Strindberg's soul. Suffering from nervous depletion, and in a generally weakened state of health, he adopted a deferential attitude towards Björnson, which, being foreign to his temperament, was logically bound to be followed by emancipation. Early in their intercourse Strindberg had made the characteristic discovery that he was endowed with greater knowledge and a more incisive understanding than Björnson. Björnson begged Strindberg to be less personal in his satire, apparently unconscious of the extremely personal nature of his own attacks upon the common enemy. The tie of friendship was gradually loosened and came to an abrupt end in 1884. Björnson summed up Strindberg in a letter:

"You who are warm, strong, weak ; you who are believing—suspicious, courageous—afraid, loving—hating, lyrical—prosaic . . ."

Strindberg was now strongly attracted to the views of Rousseau and Tolstoy. Art could not suffice; when the beautiful is not true, how can one write of the beautiful ? The world was full of suffering; tyranny and injustice barred the way of the soul. Back to Nature therefore. The life of the peasant, tilling his soil, was the best. *Among French Peasants*, published some years later, expressed this mood.

Socialism, internationalism, the theories of a broad and humanitarian outlook upon industrial processes of development which tend towards a more equal distribution of wealth and power, now fed Strindberg's hunger after social righteousness. He attempted to throw off national limitations; to feel and act as a European with pan-national sympathies and interests.

The peace movement presented itself to him as one of the greatest thoughts of the time. In his youth he had felt at one with the proletariat, trampled down by the hoofs of militarism. In his satirical writings the peacocks of the social fowl-yard—the proud bearers of epaulets and tinsel—had received a full share of his attention. In Switzerland he came into contact with the organised peace movement, and the result was the novel *Remorse*, a powerful analysis of the mental torture endured by a German officer who in obeying orders has caused three innocent Frenchmen to be shot. The inhumanity of war and the reality of human brotherhood are here presented in a manner which makes the story a stirring, yet delicately artistic appeal against the horrors of the battlefield. Whilst he thus placed himself in the ranks of the world's peace-makers, the struggle with the sex-problem, from which he never wholly escaped, developed into a battle, the noise of which was destined to reverberate through his whole life.

During the summer of 1884—whilst exposed to the unromantic surroundings of a Swiss mountain *pensionnat*—he wrote twelve stories of married life, to which he gave the innocuous title *Married*. They were published in Stockholm in September by Herr Bonnier, and had the effect of a bomb thrown amidst sleepy and contented people—contented to be rid of the enemy. The book was eagerly read by everyone, by the high priests of morality as well as by libertines; it sent shudders of indignation through the respectability which covers vice and sin with silence and called forth shouts of delight from the champions of "free" morals. It was denounced as indecent, and as a grave danger to the youth of Sweden by representatives of religion and education. The Queen of Sweden read the book and came to the conclusion that it was injurious to morality and offensive to religion. She was undoubtedly sincere in her condemnation, whilst the majority who joined the hue and cry against Strindberg were but tainted reflections of the purity upon which they prided themselves. This time the author of *The Red Room* and *The New Kingdom* had placed himself within reach of the law. Within a fortnight of the publication of *Married* the book was impounded, and proceedings were instituted against the publisher.

But it was not the indecency which was the subject of legal proceedings. It was the sacrilegious handling of Holy Communion in the first story, entitled "The Reward of Virtue," which afforded the opportunity for legal repression. True to the irreverent impulse which owed its origin to the ecclesiastical preparations in the sexton's kitchen, Strindberg had vented his feelings of opposition to the tenets of Christianity in a tasteless sentence. It recorded the commercial value of the wafers and the wine and ridiculed the " insolent fraud," which enabled the priest to foist these articles of commerce on the congregation as the flesh and blood of the " agitator " who was executed more than 1800 years ago.

The story, which to a great extent was autobiographical, dealt with the alleged evils of chastity in a youth and consequent declination of mental faculties. The problems of puberty which Wedekind subsequently dramatised with tragic force in *Frühlings Erwachen*, were amongst the painful experiences which Strindberg dwelt upon in his autobiography. In *Married* the conflict between Nature and virtue is falsely presented. The auxiliary influences of moral and physical culture are ignored.

Some stories treat of love and marriage, of the transformation of raptures and idylls into painful struggles for the maintenance of the family, of helpless young men captured in the economic trap of matrimony, of the monotony of daily domestic drudgery which makes fretful wives and impatient husbands out of ardent Romeos and dreamy Juliets. There are squabbles and reconciliations, there are scenes and *intérieurs* in the comedy of marriage to which the stories bear witness with little regard for the usual restraint of description. The characters are life-like types of Swedish middle-class society. They have been drawn with a realism which shows them as the pathetic puppets of marital fate, or as the unreflecting fools of sexual idealism. There is the deft touch of Maupassant in the rendering of love's irony, there is the inevitableness of Balzac and—in the " indecencies "—not a little of Boccaccio's mirth of imagination.

(49)

D

AUGUST STRINDBERG

When the news of the action against the publisher of *Married* reached Strindberg in Switzerland, he hesitated as to the right course to pursue. He considered the charge of blasphemy to be merely a peg on which his enemies had hung their long-suppressed lust for revenge. The efforts to suppress the book as a pornographic publication had proved futile and absurd and had served to show well-intentioned people that realism is not necessarily rank immorality. He resented the attack on freedom of religious thought. On discovering that the Swedish law punishes denial of the pure Lutheran doctrine with two years' hard labour, he reflected that, if the law were enforced, Jews, Roman Catholics, Unitarians, Methodists and Baptists would all be sent to prison. To plead guilty to the charge of blasphemy was to admit the existence of a legitimate censorship on thought and religious conviction, which he denied. But the publisher was in danger of being punished, and Strindberg could not stand by whilst a scapegoat suffered the penalty of his transgressions. A letter of protest against the proceedings had been ignored. Another letter to the authorities, in which Strindberg formally admitted his authorship, was followed by the request that he should appear personally in Court. A consultation in Geneva with Herr Bonnier, junior, followed, and as there seemed little doubt that the publisher would be found guilty, if the author shirked his responsibilty for any motive whatever, Strindberg left for Stockholm.

He received warnings on the way, gloomy prophecies that the prisoner's cell was the ultimate destination of his journey. On arriving at Stockholm on October 18th, he was met at the station by an inquisitive and admiring crowd. There were cries for a speech as he stepped out of the train amid cheers. Did this mean that there were friends as well as enemies awaiting him? He was not, after all, a *vox clamantis in deserto*. There were supporters and sympathisers ready for his message. Standing on the platform, amid the bustle and noise of the station, he addressed the people on the meaning and object of his realism. Within a few minutes he experienced the vicissitudes of the "leader" of a movement: acclaimed by some and insulted by others, he reached his hotel opposite the station amidst the excitement which is meat unto the agitator and dross to the thinker.

In the evening there was a special performance of *The Journey of Lucky Peter* which the author was invited to attend. At the theatre he was the centre of interest, the object of inquisitive glances. The public cheered him again—was it possible that he too had a following, a circle of responsive souls willing to stand by him in the struggle for new thought? But no, the sceptic within him did not believe in this adulation. "No, I am no good as a 'great' man," he reflected. "I can never learn to believe in cheers. They cheer to-day and boo to-morrow!"

During the weeks that followed he had ample opportunity for philosophical studies of the cheering-booing propensity of human nature. The violent attacks in the conservative press had all the psychological elements of the booing which is an essential stimulus to continued self-satisfaction and placid Phariseeism; the cheering which echoed from another quarter was not always attuned to the highest aspirations of the hero of the moment.

The trial of the case was painful to Strindberg. He had none of the qualities which make men revel

(51)

in loud publicity. Despite the character of his writings and the war which he had waged with his pen he had all the personal reserve of the sensitive and the recluse. On November 17th the jury brought a verdict of " Not guilty " against the author and publisher of *Married*. His friends cheered, working men in the street cheered and triumphantly escorted Strindberg to his hotel. The victory over the enemies of " free speech " was celebrated in the evening by a banquet, and on the following day Strindberg left Stockholm for Geneva, where he joined his wife.

In Sweden the controversy ran high. *Married* was once more on sale. It was stated that no less than 3,500 copies of the book had been sold during the short interval between the day of publication and the confiscation.

The advertisement provided by the prosecution now ensured the widest publicity for the book. Pedagogues and moralists saw a grave danger to the youth of Sweden in the circulation of the book.

There is a great difference in Strindberg's attitude towards women in the first and second volumes of *Married*. In the preface to the first volume Strindberg, though protesting against the " sickly " cult of woman for which Ibsen was responsible (he calls Ibsen the famous Norwegian blue-stocking), presents his scheme for the future regeneration of woman under the title of *Woman's Rights*.

The first of these is the right to have the same educational advantages as man. There is to be wholesale educational reform from which class and sex differences are to be eliminated; " unnecessary " learning is to be abolished and the substitute is to be found in a universal citizen's examination—a degree of social competency requiring the arts of reading, writing, arithmetic and elementary knowledge of the laws of one's country, with appreciation of the duties and rights of citizenship. To this curriculum one living foreign language will be added, but there will not be time for much more, for " the future will require every citizen to earn his living by manual labour in accordance with the law of nature." The regeneration of woman and the reform of marriage are thus—according to August Strindberg of 1884—inseparably bound up with socialistic hopes of equality. He proclaimed *Votes for Women* as the prerogative of the enlightened woman of the future. He wrote : —

" Is anyone wiser or more fit to rule than an old mother who, through motherhood and the household, has learnt to reign and to administer ? " Through the influence of the mother, he continues, " customs and laws will be softened, for no one has learnt forgivingness as a mother, no one knows as she does how patient, how indulgent one must be with erring human children."

The second part was full of venom against woman —women were declared to be incapable of everything, lazy, mendacious, cowardly. They were not even capable of love.

No wonder Björnson wrote : " Opinions and views rest as lightly upon him as does the name upon the pig or the cow amongst the peasants."[*]

Strindberg's wife felt that his bitter railings against women were a reflection on her character as woman and wife. His changes of front caused her the deepest distress. When she heard him express contempt of views and principles which had drawn them together, and revile that which but a short

---

[*]*Strindberg's Första Hustru;* Karin Smirnoff.

time before he had appeared to venerate, she felt the ground disappear from under her feet. After a period of total abstinence, Strindberg began to drink absinthe. He was at times miserably over-wrought and irritable. The socialistic phase passed into one of Nietzschean disdain of the stupid herd, his religious beliefs into flinty atheism. The onslaught on religion, which to Siri was holy, made matrimonial life insupportable to her. It should be said that Strindberg's first wife fought bravely to make life together possible, to make both ends meet, to bring up the children rightly, to allay the too frequent tempests of their Bohemian life.

Meanwhile, the creative energy that encompassed Strindberg sought new expression and form. *The People of Hemsö*, a novel of the fishermen's life in the Baltic, fresh as the salt breeze of the sea, bright with sunshine and the jollity of a man with steady nerves, who is thoroughly at home in a boat and in a hut, was published in 1887. In 1888 *Fisher Folk* appeared, with sketches of life on an island, broadly humorous, impressive in its unaffected narrative of the struggles and ambitions of the hardy toilers among the rocks. In both books there is a wealth of descriptive power, and there is something fundamentally healthy in the figures of the common people whom he draws, a natural pathos in their vulgarity, and even in their criminality.

There are some who see exclusively *das Dämonische* in Strindberg, and who picture him as perpetually skirting precipices of moral and intellectual negation, or as a Lucifer who never emerges from consuming tongues of fire. They have nothing to say of such books as his *Sketches of Flowers and Animals* (1888). Here we meet him, a mild and patient gardener, sowing his salad and spinach, revelling in the reward

which his cool cucumbers offer after having been
carefully tended by loving hands. Here he initiates
us into his cult of the flower, his adoration of colour
and form in the plant world; he anticipates Maeterlinck in his sensitive studies of the intelligence of
flowers and the mysteries of seeds. His *Fables* are
stories of birds, insects and bushes, betraying an
intimate knowledge of Nature, and sparkling
with a good-humoured satire. In these books there
are strokes of brilliant imagination, there is a
womanly tenderness for the lives of plant-children.
In one of his stories he tells us of a tall fir, which
can feel and suffer, and his description of the spirit
within the tree, which sobs under the wood-cutter's
axe and which some day we shall recognise, reminds
us of Fiona Macleod's *Cathal of the Woods.*
Strindberg's love of Nature had many qualities in
common with Thoreau—there is the same pleasure
in cultivating the cabbage-patch, the same ecstatic
contemplation of green life. Thoreau could find his
way in the wood during the night by the touch of
his feet. Strindberg, treading his way through the
forest in the dark hours, knew whether he walked
on soil, clubmoss or maidenhair " through the nerves
of his large toe."

The series of Strindberg's naturalistic plays, *The
Father* (1887), *Lady Julie* (1888), *Comrades* (1888),
Creditors (1890), were amongst the first plays to be
produced at M. André Antoine's Théatre Libre in
Paris. The time was one of revolt against old-
fashioned theatricality. He had the satisfaction of
being played in Paris before Ibsen. Zola wrote a
prefatory letter to the French edition of *The Father.*
Zola stated that *The Father* was one of the few
dramatic works which had the power of moving him
deeply. In a critical appreciation of Strindberg,

published in 1894, Georg Brandes praised *The Father*
as a tragedy of concentrated energy, magnificent in
its composition and powerful in its effect. " There
is something eternal in *The Father*," he wrote,
" an unforgettable psychology of woman, showing
typically feminine weakness and vice." Brandes
thought the symbolism of the final scene, in which
the man of intellect is ruined by woman, inherently
true. He added : " The strength of the imagination
and the hatred which have produced the drama are
impressive. This tragedy is a cry of anguish which
clings to one's memory, which grips and terrifies
through the depth of the passionate suffering that
uttered the cry."

I do not think that Strindberg's *The Father* has
ever found a more poignant and true interpretation
than that given in London in 1927 by Mr. Robert
Loraine. *The Father* was played in Copenhagen in
1889, and in Berlin Strindberg's plays were given at
the Freie Bühne in 1893. I shall not attempt in
this small sketch to give a complete account of the
plays. *Lady Julie* was the most successful of
Strindberg's naturalistic dramas. There is again the
struggle between man and woman, here the opposites
of class and blood are added to those of sex. In
Lady Julie Strindberg sketched the useless, unnatural,
pleasure-loving, hysterical woman of the leisured
classes whom he detested. Her surrender to the valet
is unpardonable from the point of view of society.

We cannot imagine a drama by Strindberg in which
tragedy is woven out of the misconduct of a Lord
Julius instead of a Lady Julie. A young " blood,"
neurotic, suffering from ennui, and seeking temporary
distraction in the company of Jeanne, the valet's
daughter, would not have inspired a naturalistic
drama of sex and caste. There is a wealth of material

which can be used to *épater le bourgeois* in the idea
of a well-bred woman's precipitous "return to
nature." The commonplace spectacle of a similar
descent on the part of a well-bred man affords none.

Comrades is a four-act drama of marriage, about
woman as the rival of man, Strindberg's *bête noire*.
Bertha had short hair—Strindberg did not like
women with short hair—the sight of such women
upset his equanimity. One wonders if he would have
been able to support life at all in the year 1928 !
Bertha was to Strindberg the New Woman—a
creature to be shunned and exterminated. *Creditors*
is one of the most powerful of Strindberg's plays.
It has been produced by the Stage Society. *The
Stronger* has also been performed in London. The
plays by Strindberg which have been seen in
London are nearly all of his naturalistic period.
Of the remainder of the fifty-one plays, by which
he has encompassed many " schools " of playwriting,
evolved new dramatic forms, and tested different
methods of expression, the British public knows
little or nothing.

Naturalism has passed away. The shallow
materialism, the false simplicity of presentation,
with which it sought to kill romantic methods of
dramaturgy, proved fatal. They were found to be
as unreal as the old-fashioned conventions of the
stage. But there were other qualities in the movement which have not died, but profoundly influenced
the character-drawing and scenic development of the
modern drama. Hauptmann, Hervieu, Wedekind,
Schnitzler, Gorky, Tchekhov have transmuted and
individualised the permanent elements of the early
realism.

As an exponent of naturalism Strindberg's personality towered high above the first noisy purveyors

of what M. Jullien named " slices of life "—some
distressingly indigestible. It is true that the fabric
of his drama was woven out of the ever-recurring
theme of sexual antagonism. He described it with
the undertone of personal suffering—the suffering
of experience and of pity—with which Tolstoy made
his peasants articulate in *Powers of Darkness*, or
Henry Becque the ill-used women in *Les Corbeaux*.

Strindberg's plays are honestly unpleasant. They
differ from the popular play of amorous escapades
and half-uttered indecencies as the mountain torrent
differs from the garden fountain. They are written
by the impelling force of an idea, whilst the conventional immorality play exists in the interests of
frivolous entertainment.

And do they not, after all, treat of " love," the
obsessing object of dramatic interest from the
plaintive demi-monde of Dumas *fils* to the man-
hunting Ann of Bernard Shaw ? From Sudermann
and Pinero to Schnitzler and Capus, through
sentimentalism, conventionalism, and cynicism, the
theme persists in absorbing dramatic imagination.
Compared with Schnitzler, the prince of amorists,
Strindberg's *milieu* is sombre with fateful retribution.
In *Lady Julie* and *Creditors*, both one-act plays and
each with only three speaking parts, he created a
new dramatic form. He now assailed the old theatre
with the same vigour with which he had attacked
old social institutions.

" The reproach," wrote Strindberg, " was levelled
against my tragedy, *The Father*, that it was so sad,
as though one wanted merry tragedies. People
clamour for the joy of life, and theatrical managers
order farces, as though the joy of life consisted in
being foolish, and in describing people as if they

were each and all afflicted with St. Vitus' Dance or idiocy. I find the joy of life in the powerful, cruel struggle of life, and my enjoyment in discovering something, in learning something. Therefore I have chosen an unusual, though instructive, case; in other words, an exception, but a great exception, which confirms the rule, and which is sure to offend the lovers of the banal."

The transformation of the diffuse drama in many acts into the concise and dynamic one-act play, with few characters and the simplification of stage technique, were the salient points in Strindberg's proclamation of Theatre Reform. He held that there is generally but one scene, towards which the playwright mounts by devious paths, and that author and audience alike are made to endure painful side-shows for the sake of one thing worth seeing.

The scenery should be simple. "With the aid of a table and two chairs the strongest conflicts which life offers could be presented," he writes of the *genre* of the *proverbe*, " and by that form of art it became possible to popularise the discoveries of modern psychology." The decorations should only be suggestive of place and time. An impressionistic representation of a corner of a room and its furniture —not the whole room—is all that is needed. Grotesque scene-painting should be abolished together with the stagey villain, who can create no illusion of wickedness.

In writing of the all-important subject of characterisation Strindberg pointed out (preface to *Lady Julie*) that he drew his modern characters vaccillating, broken, mixtures of old and new. . . " My souls (characters) are conglomerations of past and present stages of culture, scraps of books and newspapers, fragments of men and women, torn shreds of Sunday attire that are now rags, such as go to make up a soul."

He ridicules the ordinary idea of a strong character. The person " who has acquired a fixed temperament or accommodated himself to a certain rôle in life, who in a word has ceased to grow, was supposed to have character ; whilst one who developed, the skilful navigator on the stream of life who does not sail with close-tied sheets, but who knows when to fall off before the wind and when to luff again, was deemed deficient in character. . . . This bourgeois conception of the fixity of the soul was transferred to the stage, where all that is bourgeois has ever reigned supreme. Such a character became synonymous with a gentleman, fixed and ready-made, one who invariably appeared drunk, jocular, melancholy. . . . I do not, therefore, believe in simple theatrical characters."

He repudiates the summary judgments which dramatists pass on human beings, and tells us that "vice has an obverse which shows a considerable likeness to virtue."

The secret of Strindberg's great influence on the theatre lay in this very conception of character. His men and women are *alive*, moving, changing, growing, shrinking in ceaseless response to the pressure of existence. He is the dramatist of the *perpetuum mobile* in the modern heart, the interpreter of inexhaustible discontent in himself and others. His personality vibrates in the dialogue, and lifts the idea of the play to the surface in every consecutive scene, but the artist in him is stronger than the ideologue. The curtain and the settled problem do not drop together. Strindberg has answered a question or two, tentatively, in his own manner, but others crowd in upon him and his audience. The absence of finality is felt through the tragic endings, through the strong blend of moods, emotions and desires of his exceptional characters, through the unreasonableness of his prejudices. In spite of pessimism and cynicism a hope of change is communicated to the spectator, which penetrates depression and stimulates the curiosity to live.

Amongst the one-act plays which were written between 1887-97, *Samum, Pariah, The Stronger, Playing with Fire* and *The Link* present the typical characters of psychic intensity and neuropathic activity. *Pariah* is a dialogue which bears the mark of the master-craftsman in the dramatic presentation of psychological events. It is a contest of minds founded on a tale by Ola Hansson.

The Stronger is a contest of temperaments carried out by one voice only. Two women—the wife and the mistress of one man—have met in a café. Mademoiselle Y. sits silent, whilst Madame X. talks. But her silence conveys more than speech. *Playing with Fire* is a triangular comedy of marriage, in which conjugal fidelity is saved at the eleventh hour through sudden and truly Strindbergian disillusionment which makes the friend of husband and wife depart like a rocket from the house of temptation, whilst the peace of an orderly lunch descends upon the family. *The First Warning* is a conjugal squabble, and one of the weakest dramatic episodes conceived by Strindberg.

The Link, a tragedy published in 1897, is a masterly divorce-court scene. Here Strindberg draws the shame and agony of the broken marriage with bitter realism, and yet with a delicate touch of that all-human compassion before which the flowers of satire fade. The link is the child.

Strindberg has been classified as a dramatist

whose knife was forever delving in the pathological tissues of passions and whose eyes saw nothing but the broad and sombre lines of inevitable tragedy. I have already referred to him as a gardener and a teller of fables. In preparation of his book on French peasants, Strindberg travelled through France, notebook in hand, stayed amongst the peasants, measured hay and corn, attended weddings and fairs, annotating the prices of meat and butter, studied the ravages of the phylloxera and geological formations. The book is crammed with facts and comparative statistics of town and country, wheat and wine, village education, libraries, labourers' wages, cheese-making, the best fertilisers, and other matters of import to rural economy.

He shirked no trouble, avoided no obstacles to equip himself as a writer on gigantic subjects. His encyclopædic grasp of a many-sided subject is shown in this book, and in his numerous essays on sociological questions. It carries with it a certain superficiality and readiness to theorise from insufficient data which may necessitate a graceful retraction of opinions once loudly proclaimed. But there is ample compensation in the freshness and vigour of a mind which bears crop after crop without exhausting itself. Such a quickly grown crop, verdant and luxurious in ideas, is the essay, written in 1884, *On the General Discontent, its Causes and Remedies,* in which he inveighs against the evils of a false culture, and within the space of a hundred pages lets Society pass in review before his critical pen.

Though the mists of Nietzscheanism lie heavily over *At the Edge of the Sea* written in 1890, Mr. Edmund Gosse was in error in describing Strindberg as " the most remarkable creative talent started by the philosophy of Nietzsche." Strindberg was certainly

not " started " by Nietzsche, who was entirely unknown to him until the autumn of 1888, when Georg
Brandes brought the two writers together. A
correspondence between Nietzsche and Strindberg
began in 1889, and continued until Nietzsche's illness.
Nietzsche read Strindberg's novels with interest, and
Strindberg duly acknowledged the influence which
Nietzsche exercised upon him, but protested against
the mistaken view that he was made by Nietzsche.

The statement that Strindberg was a Nietzschean
pur et simple is as absurd as the statement that he
was a Darwinist or a Methodist. He passed through
the fatalism of Hartmann, the pessimism of
Schopenhauer, the naturalism of Zola, the realism
of Turgenev and Dostoevsky. On one occasion he
speaks of Balzac as his master, on another he calls
himself a Voltairean. These influences are but lights
on the way. He passes on, and speaks to us with a
new tongue. When charged with inconsistency he
might well have answered with Walt Whitman : " I
am large—I contain multitudes."

In 1890 Strindberg's first marriage was dissolved.
It was preceded by a crescendo of accusations on
his part, of mutual misery, of vain attempts to mend
broken strings. The story of Siri von Essen's life in
Finland, of her brave struggle to maintain the
children during the years when Strindberg contributed
little or nothing, has been told by their daughter
in the book to which I have already referred.

There was much hostility to Strindberg in Sweden
during the years which followed the prosecution in
connection with *Married.* When yachting along
the west coast for the purpose of collecting material
for a great work on *The Scenery of Sweden,* he was
actually refused permission to land in one of the
fishing villages. During the two years which he

now spent in Sweden he became embittered by the enmity of his critics. He isolated himself on one of his beloved islands outside Stockholm, wrote and painted. In the autumn of 1892 an exhibition of his pictures was held in Stockholm. It was impressions of the sea which his brush had chosen—ice, mist, storm—and painted, not only with a tender feeling for island scenery, but disclosing considerable technical merit and accuracy of hand.*

In the autumn of 1892 we find Strindberg in Germany. The curse of marriage is no longer upon his head. He lives at Friedrichshagen, near Berlin, with his friends, the Swedish writer Ola Hansson and his wife Laura Marholm, who has written an interesting psychological study of Strindberg. Strindberg has passed through one of those " deaths," in which he found temporary Nirvana, when the battle of thoughts had been too sanguinary. He has forsaken literature, thrown away the pen as a worthless tool of a tormented imagination, which can scratch but not solve the riddle of the Sphinx. He has been re-born—a scientist. The exact sciences—chemistry, physics, astronomy—hold out hopes of complete replies to questions which the playwright can dress in human shape but not analyse.

Strindberg's friend, Gustaf Uddgren, has described a visit to him at this time. His study was bare and uninviting. On the floor there lay stacks of scientific books piled up against the wall. They had been bought with the first money he had earned in Germany, and none had been wasted on the luxury of a bookcase. The room contained a large, old easel,

---

* In *The Strindberg I Knew* Birger Mörner publishes a letter from Strindberg—pathetic in its simplicity: "' I am now a painter in Paris; have sold for 400 fr. I paint small decorative panneaux on cardboard. Have 10 ready. The price is 35 kr. each, with gilt frame."

not unlike a brown skeleton; a writing-table, from which the usual heaps of manuscript and notes were conspicuously absent; and, for the comfort of the body, a few easy chairs and a sofa, arranged so as to give the impression of a drawing-room. Strindberg did not wish to discuss literary subjects. He was glad to have left off writing, and looked forward with eager joy to scientific research. Uddgren tried in vain to induce him to talk about Walt Whitman. Strindberg preferred to discuss Red Indians with his guest, who knew something of the wild west.

After a few months at Friedrichshagen, Strindberg moved to Berlin. He was in need of change and expansion. In the evenings he was now found in a little Wein Stube in Unter den Linden, which is called " Zum Schwarzen Ferkel," which had already won fame as the favourite resort of Heine and E. T. A. Hoffmann. Here he was the centre of a literary and scientific coterie. Guitar in hand, amidst sympathetic friends, he became Dionysus, the singer of glad tidings, of wine-born joy. He improvised songs, and the nights were made short with wit and sparkling discussions.

Amongst other friends of the coterie were Holger Drachmann, Gunnar Heiberg, Adolf Paul, and Edvard Munch.

It was at this period that Strindberg was drawn to the study of alchemy, astrology, magic, magnetism and spiritism.

Whilst literary Berlin was acclaiming Strindberg as the naturalistic playwright, his mind was centred on the hyperchemical speculations which later on found expression in his *Antibarbarus I or the Psychology of Sulphur or All is in All*, and in *Sylva Sylvarum*.

Wings of imagination were lifting him to new planes of thought, but there was a sudden jerk on the

chain which bound him to earth. He fell in love.
The ideal woman had again appeared in the person
of Frida Uhl, a young Austrian girl, daughter of
Hofrath Friedrich Uhl, in Vienna. They became
engaged, and art-loving Berlin was one day surprised
to see Strindberg escorting his fiancée to the National
Gallery. He was attired in the fashionable apparel
of the Berlin dandy. They were married in April,
1893, and spent their honeymoon at Gravesend. An
injunction had meanwhile been granted against the
German Edition of *The Confession of a Fool*. The
prosecution failed. Strindberg and his wife spent the
winter at her father's country place at Armstädten,
on the Danube, where he returned to his esoteric
studies, and wrote his *Antibarbarus*. In August, 1894,
Strindberg went to Paris accompanied by his wife.
Their child was left in Austria. The tie was now
irksome to him; *les hautes études* and not woman
had again become mistress of his soul. In November
he sent his wife back to her parents.

"It was with a feeling of wild joy," he writes,
"that I returned from Gare du Nord, where I had
left my dear little wife who was going to our child
who had fallen ill in a distant country. The sacrifice
of my heart was thus made complete." Their last
words "When do we meet again?—Soon," were
deceptive; an intuition truly told him that they had
parted for ever. He had placed human affection on
the altar of truth-seeking, thus practising the motto
with which *Inferno* opens:

> Courbe la tête, fier Sicambre!
> Adore ce que tu as brûlé,
> Brûle ce que tu as adoré!

At the Café de la Régence he sat down at the table
where he used to sit with his wife, "the beautiful

wardress of my prison who spied on my soul day and night, guessed my secret thoughts, watched the course of my ideas, jealously observed my spirit's striving towards the unknown." He felt free, a sense of mental expansion, of liberated power, a call to reach the arcanum of human knowledge.

This fear of an alien invasion of the soul made Strindberg flee again and again from the prison-house of love. In all his books the love between man and woman is a duel of love and hatred. Repulsion follows attraction. His couples, auto-biographical or purely imaginary, burn in the fires of love-hatred. After some time love always became irksome to Strindberg. He wanted male companion-ship, felt a woman's love to be like a vampire sucking his mind.

In Paris he was now the playwright of the day. The success of *Lady Julie* and *Creditors* was followed by a brilliant performance of *The Father* at Théâtre de l'Œuvre in December. All Paris talked of his originality and of his misogyny which provided a piquant sensation and a subject for interesting gossip in literary and dramatic circles. He was interviewed and photographed—he was the *cher maître* of the theatrical manager who expected from him a sensible appreciation of his possibilities for further triumphs on the stage. In Berlin he was the literary lion of the moment. His plays and novels lay in the book-sellers' windows in attractive German dress, his portrait was exhibited, his personality was discussed. He was saluted as a leader of a new movement. But he turned his back on all this. Another self was shed; a voice within whispered the old burning " Beyond this "—drove him across the borderland of sanity, and into the chaos of unhuman desires.

He left the café, and returned to his rooms in

AUGUST STRINDBERG

Quartier Latin. From their hiding-place in his trunk he took six crucibles made of fine porcelain, bought with money which he "had stolen from himself," made up a fierce fire in the stove, and pulled down the blinds for the night's experiment. He tested his theory regarding the composition of sulphur. Experiments were conducted night after night. His hands were burnt with the intense heat of his sulphur flames. The skin fell off in flakes, but joy in the pursuit of the problems was greater than the pain. He wrote love-letters to his wife relating to her the wonderful discoveries which he had made. She replied by warnings against such futile and foolish occupations. Irritated by her want of sympathy, Strindberg sent her a letter of farewell to wife and child, in which he led her to understand that a love affair had absorbed all his thoughts. She replied by instituting proceedings for divorce.

The charge which he had made against himself was not true, and he was soon the prey of remorse. On Christmas Eve the vision of his deserted wife and child by the Christmas tree caused him to flee from the company, which he had sought, and visit café after café, where he failed to find comfort in the usual glass of absinthe. During the night the feeling of being persecuted by an unknown power, bent on preventing his great task, overcame him. He slept badly and was repeatedly awakened by a cold current of air sweeping across his face. Poverty, his persistent enemy, did not leave him in peace. He lacked the necessary means to pay for rent and regular meals. His hands were black and swollen through neglect, and symptoms of blood-poisoning in the arms set in. The news of his helplessness and misery spread amongst his countrymen in Paris. He was sought out by a persistent countrywoman who raised a sum of money amongst the Swedes in Paris, and Strindberg was brought to the Hospital of Saint Louis, his cup of humiliation filled to overflowing.

Recovered, he continued his chemical studies and became a student at the Sorbonne, where he used the analytical library.

Strange feelings and symptoms developed. He became conscious of unseen presences. A sense of being persecuted made itself manifest. There were inexplicable noises in his room, delusions began to crowd in upon him. Strange dreams foretold the future, common-place objects assumed fantastic shape. One day, when looking at the embryo of a sprouting walnut under the microscope, he saw two little white hands folded as if in prayer. Immovable, perfect in form, they were there, the hands of a child or a woman raised beseechingly towards him. There were other mysteries. The coal in his stove burned itself into grotesque shapes, works of some kind of elemental sculptor, which were so realistic that the sparrows, feeding on crumbs by his window, were frightened by the sight of them.

One night, after a festive evening with friends, he was received by the devil himself in correct middle-age attire, thus competing with Blake, who, one day, whilst ascending the stairs of his house, saw Satan glaring at him through a window.

From sulphur he turned to iodine as a subject of original experimentation, and then, oblivious of Aristotle's injunctions, to the goldmaker's art. He rejected the alchemical faith that gold alone is free from sulphur, and commenced experiments with solutions of sulphate of iron in support of the theory that gold contains iron and sulphur. He succeeded in making gold—his special gold of art—but it vanished when put to the ordinary chemical test. Signs and guidance from unseen Powers encouraged him to persist in spite of failure.

But the spirit of gold is fickle. One day, after repeated failures, when standing naked to the waist, as a smith, before the fiercely burning furnace, he looked into the crucible, and saw a skull with a pair of glittering eyes. The eyes looked into his soul with a supernatural irony, and the goldmaker was struck by paralysing doubt, by fear of the consequences of his folly.

He was tormented by unrest, shame and doubt—longing to find spiritual security. He went "mad." Mad as Tasso and Cellini, Poe and Blake. We cannot dispute the madness, but we may hold that the madness of genius is more valuable to humanity than the sanity of mediocrity.

In Strindberg we can clearly distinguish between cerebral derangements causing auditory hallucinations as well as delusions of persecution, and the super-conscious activity which produced the state of *clair-psychism*, which is generally classed with insanity. Dr. W. Hirsch studied Strindberg's disease from the ordinary alienist's point of view, and concluded that he suffered from *paranoia simplex chronica*—a diagnosis which is empty of meaning when applied to such a mind. Dr. S. Rahmer made Strindberg the subject of a more comprehensive psychopathic study, and defined his case as one of *melancholia dæmomaniaca*. The inadequacy of such diagnosis will be apparent to every serious student of *Inferno* and *Legends*—the books which are mostly extracts from the diary in which he recorded his madness—and of plays like *To Damascus*, *Advent*, *Easter*, *The Dream Play*, and *The Great Highway*,

which give evidence of his lucidity, and of the
knowledge which he distilled from mental torture.

There is nothing original in the fact that a man
describes his own madness in prose or verse. Such
descriptions may even be regarded as a distinct genre
of literary activity, perverse and detestable to those
who want only the " cheerful " note in literature,
but of infinite interest to those who place a truthful
account of the human soul above one which is
pleasing. Nathaniel Lee's poems, Lenan's *Traum-
gewalten*, Hoffmann's *Kreisler* possess a psychological
interest which no clamour for literary cradle-songs
can remove. Strindberg's self-revelations have a
touch of that exultation which, through a dominant
curiosity, survives the most complete cheerlessness,
horror, and pain—that joy of which Charles Lamb
wrote to Coleridge: " Dream not, Coleridge, of
having tasted all the grandeur and wildness of fancy
till you have gone mad," and which made him look
back upon his lunacy " with a gloomy kind of envy."

Through tortures of mind, through fears and
hallucinations, the defiant atheist in Strindberg died.
He had been conscious of the presence of demons ;
he also became conscious of the presence of angels.
He found Swedenborg and a whole new philosophy
of spiritual evolution. He returned to the Bible of
his youth with a new interest. There were moments
when he laboured under a sense of guilt, other
moments when he felt drawn away from life by a
heavenly nostalgia. Of such moments he writes :
" I despise the earth, this impure and unworthy
world, humanity and the works of humanity. I see
in myself the righteous man to whom the Almighty
has sent trials, and whom the purgatory of earthly
life shall make worthy of approaching deliverance."

In the course of a long talk with Strindberg during

this period, Uddgren could find no signs of brain-softening. The mania, the eccentricities, the flashing imagination, the instinct for self-martyrisation were there intensified, but not the incoherency which he had observed in other literary friends who were victims of insanity. It is also remarkable that throughout Strindberg's period of madness his writings were accepted and printed.

Strindberg underwent treatment in Sweden, and gradually the fears, the sense of the demon which sucked his heart, the sinister voices and signs retreated.

He had seen human souls sanctified by a catholic mysticism which brought humility and fortitude. The symbols, the certainty, the rich imagery of the Catholic Church had appealed to him when the poverty of philosophical speculation had made him despair of human intelligence. One day an image of the Madonna, carried through the streets of Paris on a cart following a hearse, had strangely attracted him. Like Tasso's vision of the Virgin in the midst of his feverish torment by noises and tinkling bells, Strindberg's gaze on the image of all-merciful motherhood brought comfort. At first attracted to Catholic prayers, and to the ideal of the monastic life by the instinct which makes the man in pain seek an anodyne, he was gradually led to a realisation of the depths of esoteric Christianity.

Strindberg's early blasphemies and atheism were the fruits of an inverted sense of religion which left him no peace. His devotional mood could find no bridge of union with his scientific mood. The search for knowledge and the search for God led to different goals. A theosophical friend now sent him Madame Blavatsky's *Secret Doctrine*, which Strindberg criticised severely, though he knew that his outspokenness

AUGUST STRINDBERG

w*o*uld deprive him of a friend and a benefactor. He declined to join a " sect " which denied a personal God, the only one who could satisfy his religious needs. He declared Madame Blavatsky's masterpiece to be "detestable, through the conscious and unconscious deceptions and the stories of the existence of Mahatmas," interesting, through the quotations from little-known authors, condemnable, above all, as the work of " a gynander who has desired to outdo man, and who pretends to have over-thrown science, religion, philosophy, and to have placed a priestess of Isis on the altar of the crucified One."

In spite of this denunciation, Strindberg had absorbed many theosophical ideas, and his later writings are not altogether free from the influence of the despised " gynander," and the theories of occult science which she expounded.

His wish to see his child was gratified through an invitation from his wife to come to Austria. He stayed with her mother and aunt, two pious and gentle old women, who treated his soul-sickness with Christian forbearance and healing sympathy. He did not meet his wife.

He was still subject to "astral" attacks, to "electric" discharges, to nightmares and ghostly visitations. He was as yet unable to bring about order in the unruly house of his mind. Whether we use spiritualistic language and call him a medium, or that of psycho-logy and label the messages which reached him " teleological automatism," there can be no doubt that he had a hyper-sensitiveness which made him a lightning-conductor for the psychic currents of his time. We may turn away with disdain from the pitiful picture of Strindberg at his writing table, warding off the imaginary attacks of elementals, incubi, lamiæ, by thrusts in the air with a Dalmatian dagger. But that there were within him cryptopsychic gifts of telepathy, clair-audience, and divination, a consciousness of a reality other than that which is cognisable to the senses, no student of psychic forces can doubt.

In December, 1896, Strindberg went to Sweden. Swedenborg's *Arcana Cœlestia,* which he now read, dissipated his fears of persecution by showing him that all the horrors, through which he had passed, were recognised by Swedenborg as incidental to that purgation of soul which is the highest object of life. Strindberg found that, before receiving his moment-ous revelations, Swedenborg had passed through nightly tortures resembling his own. By informing him of the real nature of the horrors Swedenborg liberated him from the electricians, the black magicians, the destroyers, the jealous gold-makers, and the fear of madness. " He has shown me the only path to salvation: to seek out the demons in their dens within myself, and to kill them . . . through repentance."

Inferno was composed in Lund, the little University town in the south of Sweden, between May 3rd and June 25th, 1897. *Legends,* which is but a rifacimento of the struggle to slay the " demons in their dens," was begun in Lund, and finished in Paris in October, 1897. In March, 1898, Strindberg went back to Lund, free from haunting obsessions of evil, master of his madness, enriched by religious experiences which produced an exuberant rise of new ideas. He had crossed the Rubicon. Henceforth he shared in that direct vision which makes paralysing doubt impos-sible, and which is the prerogative of " God's fools " all over the world. To the end of life his mind retained intellectual disquiet; there remained in him

a strain of the wild man, an over-balance of curiosity
which set up eternal enmity between him and convention. The Swedish critic, Oscar Levertin, succinctly
summed up Strindberg in the Italian proverb: *All
soul, all gall, all fire.* But after 1898 there is a calm
light which the unruly flames cannot hide. His
spiritual wrestlings continue through the zenith of
his literary production, but they leave him stronger.

There is a striking resemblance between Swedenborg
and Strindberg in versatility of mood and thought.
To Swedenborg he dedicates his first *Blue Book*
(1907) in the following words: "To Emanuel
Swedenborg, Teacher and Leader, this book is
dedicated by the Disciple." The *Blue Book* deals
with every thinkable subject—religious, philosophical, scientific—in an aphoristic and combative
manner which is pervaded by a curious mixture
of pride and humility. Here speaks the High
Priest of Knowledge, here quivers the helpless
embryo of the humanity which is to come. In these
motley pages the Teacher and the Disciple talk of
telepathy, chemistry, astronomy, meteorology, spectral
analysis, atoms and crystals, the psychology of plants,
the secrets of birds, the formation of clouds, Dar-
winism, radium, woman, the secrets of chess, the
secrets and magic of numbers, the Mesopotamian
language, hieroglyphics, Hebraic research, symbolism,
clairvoyance, and a hundred other subjects.

To the Swedenborgian and eighteenth-century
conception of the natural world and the spiritual
world Strindberg added the craving for a synthetic
interpretation of facts, which was characteristic of the
nineteenth century, and which had found its foremost
representatives in Spencer and Comte. In his sense
of truth, in his work for the correlation of knowledge,
in his readiness to forsake pleasant beliefs for

unpleasant facts, Strindberg realised Swedenborg's description of a certain phase of angelic life: "To grow old in heaven is to grow young."

The mystery of personality metamorphosis, of primary and secondary individualities, contained within the frame of one human body, is now a recognised subject of inquiry in the domain of abnormal psychology. In a preface to *The Author*, written in 1909, Strindberg says of himself as the writer of the book twenty years earlier: "The personality of the author is just as much a stranger to me as to the reader—and just as unsympathetic."

Alone was the dulcet autobiographical *finale* to the *agitato* of *Inferno*.

To the natural capacity for suffering was added that imposed on him through the development of his psychic powers. He did not only live the lives of others "telepathically"; his sensibility became so exteriorised as to receive impressions at a great distance. Thus he used to feel, when one of his plays was being performed for the first time in some part of Europe, though he had received no information in regard to the performance. In 1907 he told Uddgren that, after going to bed at ten in the evening, he was sometimes awakened by the sound of loud applause which caused him to sit up in bed, wondering if he was in a theatre. Such a telepathic ovation was invariably followed by the news of some dramatic success. In the first *Blue Book*, "the Disciple" relates the following: "In a company I interrupted myself with a smile in the middle of an animated conversation. 'What are you smiling at?' asked someone. 'The southern express pulled up at the Central Station just now,' was the reply. Another time something similar happened, and I said: 'The curtain has now fallen on the last act in Helsingfors, and I heard the applause after my first night.' "

The most remarkable passage in the *Blue Book* is perhaps the following summary of his *clairpsychism* :

" I feel at a distance when somebody touches my fate, when enemies threaten my personal existence, but also when people speak kindly of me or wish me well ; I feel in the street, if I meet friend or enemy; I have participated in the suffering caused by an operation on a person towards whom I feel comparatively indifferent; I have twice gone through the death agony of others with attendant physical and mental suffering; the last time I passed through three diseases in six hours, and rose well when the absent one had been liberated through death. This makes life painful, but rich and interesting."

Strindberg's fiftieth birthday was celebrated quietly in Lund in 1899. A general feeling of distrust and bewilderment was prevalent amongst his countrymen, though he was not without friends of influence and understanding. At the age of fifty he had returned to Sweden, apparently healthy in mind and body, in the prime of life, charged with a literary vitality which confounded current theories of his insanity. He had calmly and unostentatiously resumed his task of writing drama. The haunted, feverish expression had left his countenance; he had made himself a new visage, upon which were stamped self-mastery and power. And, yet, he had recently published *Inferno* and *Legends,* and laid bare his soul's misery and delirium in throbbing pages, over which the reviewers had poured acrid contempt. He had written *To Damascus* in a gust of mediæval repentance, and uncovered himself in the transports of asceticism. With a sigh of relief his enemies

AUGUST STRINDBERG

had laid aside their opposition to his indiscretions
and revelations, his materialism and transcenden-
talism, his socialism and individualism. They felt
that there was no need to take a lunatic seriously.
His friends had waited patiently for the " dancing
star " which they knew would arise out of the chaos.

The Saga of the Folkungs, Gustavus Vasa and *Eric
XIV* appeared in 1899, and showed that the author
of *Master Olof* had returned to the art with which,
twenty-seven years earlier, he had given his country
its greatest historical play. With the precision of
the somnambulist who takes up the thread of mental
events, regardless of the time that has passed,
Strindberg resumed the story of *Master Olof* where
he had left off. In *Gustavus Vasa* we again meet
Olof, the renegade, but he is now—as befits his
character—a secondary person, duly subservient to
the Power of the Time, King Gustavus Vasa. With
Gustavus Vasa and *Eric XIV* Strindberg attained to
mastery of a dramatic art in which he stands
unsurpassed. The art of writing *the psychological
drama of history* is his, and his alone. No other
dramatist of modern times has approached him
in clarity of historical vision, or in imaginative
reconstruction of living characters which are at once
true to their time and to all times.

Eric XIV, the drama of the reign of the mad son
of the sane King Gustavus, is a masterpiece of life-
like presentation. Searching comparisons between
the arts of Strindberg and Shakespeare are otiose.
But in the dramatic treatment of lunacy the author
of *Eric XIV* may well be compared with the author
of *Hamlet, Lear,* and *Macbeth.* The dramatic
verisimilitude of Strindberg's lunatics is made perfect
through an experiential familiarity with the nether-

most adventures of the mind, which Shakespeare lacked. He can describe every form of mental derangement, and has not forgotten the soul obsessed by God and, therefore, detached from the world. In *The Saga of the Folkungs* the Voice of the Unseen speaks through an obsessed woman who sees the souls of people and is able to reveal the hidden treachery of those who surround King Magnus.

A row of historical plays followed: *Gustavus Adolphus* (1900); *Engelbrecht* (1901); *Charles XII* (1901); *Gustavus III* (1903); *Queen Christina* (1903); *The Nightingale of Wittenberg* (1903); *The Last Knight* (1908); *The National Director* (1909); *The Earl of Bjälbo* (1909). Of these, *Gustavus Adolphus* with its breadth of battlefield panorama; *Charles XII* with its narrow searchlight on the declining figure of the lion-hearted but beaten king; *Queen Christina* with its flamboyant sketch of the clever and capricious daughter of Gustavus Adolphus, are eminently playable. *Gustavus III* has pointed dialogue, cameo-like pictures of word-fencing; it faithfully paints the decadent time when Sweden was steeped in the sterile scepticism of France; it portrays the reaction which led to the assassination of the King of Masquerades, but the play is not woven with the dramaturgic skill of the former dramas. *The Last Knight* is an historical jugglery with ideas in five acts which strains the dramatic form beyond its measure of elasticity. The over-balance of psychological analysis mars some of the later historical dramas. It makes some of the transcendental plays and the chamber plays mere dramatic dialogues, pictures of minds in conflict; it gives us the Shadow Theatre of the Soul, and leads Strindberg to bold defiance of the rules of dramaturgy—including those laid down by himself.

AUGUST STRINDBERG

The series of plays which have been designated as symbolical, transcendental, mystical and mad—according to the mental outlook of the reader—bring us nearest to the real Strindberg, to the essential in his imaginative art which, though illusive and often completely submerged, yet stands forth as the structure of his life. To this series belong *To Damascus*, I and II (1898), *Advent* (1899), *The Dance of Death*, I and II (1901), *Easter* (1901), *The Crown Bride* (1902), *Swanwhite* (1902), *The Dream Play* (1902), *The Great Highway* (1909). In these plays we have the eternal questions of the human mind, the joys of illusion, the sorrows of knowledge, the fruits of sin and hatred, the rise through pain and suffering, the soul's battle with relentless fate, the awful mystery of existence, and the ultimate hope of something better to come, cast into the weird and haunting shapes of the people of Strindberg's inner world; the souls that are at once real and unreal, mad and sane, acting in the solid world of matter, and held in shadowy bondage by the mists of dreamland. Here we meet them all, the souls that have gone by, that are here around us, that are yet to come. They meet us with tears and smiles, with lies and truth, with virtue and vice, pathetic and repulsive, lovable and loathsome—humanity.

Strindberg suggests the soul's corruption and the soul's ineffable sweetness with the same impassioned power of creation.

The law of *karma*—the chain of cause and effect—runs through all these plays, and binds together the psychological sequence where the dramatic construction fails.

In *The Dance of Death* we have, perhaps, the most sharply chiselled dramatic form of all his later plays.

It is a symphony of married hatred and misery in which the orchestration is perfect. The dialogue is at once natural and calculated; the silent play of the piece even more intensely suggestive than the spoken words. We get glimpses of the dramatic art of bygone days: that of Æschylus, Sophocles and Euripides; we are mercilessly ground in the mill of a ghastly nineteenth-century problem play. The figure of the Captain of the Fortress, the untruthful, scheming old rascal who has attained to a diabolical mastery in the art of making others unhappy and uncomfortable, is drawn with a supreme irony which makes it unique in vital drama. Amongst Strindberg's realistic plays it has another distinction: it represents his only stage-creation of a vampire-like *husband*. The wife is naturally not far behind him. Death stands behind the central figures of the play, the dancing death of Holbein and Saint-Saëns. The strains of his tune drown the jarring notes of conflict, and bring the voice of hope to the Captain's lips: " Wipe out, and pass on ! "

It is as if the heat of imagination, which produced some of Strindberg's great books, were too great to permit him to leave a subject, when, artistically, it is finished. After *Inferno* he wrote *Legends*, which was but a faint echo. The theme of *To Damascus* is weakly repeated in *The Great Highway*, a drama in verse and prose which also deals with the soul's fearful struggle and disillusionment. *To Damascus* contains some shallow thoughts and some banalities of expression, but it is a powerful creation, magnificently conceived. In *The Great Highway* the mysticism falls flat, the play does not grip by any poetic power; it is an *olla podrida* of its author's philosophy of life which sometimes is not even lukewarm. But it does contain some gems of lyrical beauty, and one or two passages in which Strindberg reaches his own heights.

The art of Ibsen is complex, yet simple. Born out of the depths of his love of truth and his love of beauty, it arose, well-formed, palpable, a thing for all the world to see and hear, an indictment of the gigantic social fraud to which all must ultimately listen. It is essentially exoteric. So is the art of the rival and minor playwright, Björnson, who has given the world its most perfect dramatised sermons. Strindberg's art is incalculable, subtle, the caprice of a spirit that cannot exhaust itself: esoteric because it is ever rooted in the unconscious.

In versatility of dramatic form Hauptmann stands nearest Strindberg. He has almost as many strings to his harp as the Swede—he has written naturalistic plays and fairy drama, social plays and mystical drama, farce, comedy, romance and realism. Both dramatists are impelled by pity for human suffering, but the pity that guides Hauptmann, and which is typified by *The Weavers,* is an elemental, earth-bound pity, concerned with food and poverty, lack of shelter and work. Strindberg's pity is transcendentalised; it hovers round the greater mysteries of existence itself, seeks to extract the human spirit from the curse of illusion. Hence the absence of finality in his writings. No book gives the impression of being quite finished; they all transmit the ache for a new point of view. Whilst Maeterlinck has evolved a philosophy of spiritualised tranquillity, and administers a soothing narcotic for the Soul Rampant in the twilight of his charmed castles, Strindberg walks on acutely conscious of the thorns upon which he treads. Whilst Björnson, satisfied, proclaims his ideal of physical purity, and throws down *A Gauntlet* at vice, Strindberg is haunted by the ideal of the human soul's unattainable purity from dross. Whilst Bernard Shaw cuts the world's perplexities with a joke, a brilliant paradoxical joke, Strindberg raises his hands in threatening condemnation at the Godhead Himself. In Villiers de l'Isle Adam's *Elën,* Samuel says to Goetze: "Science will not suffice. Sooner or later you will end by coming to your knees." *Goetze:* "Before what?" *Samuel:* "Before the Darkness." Strindberg was brought to his knees by the Darkness, but he rose with the dawn that followed.

During the thirteen years that passed between the quiet celebration of Strindberg's fiftieth birthday and the national festivities with which the Swedish people acclaimed him on January 22nd, 1912, his countrymen were gradually made aware of his greatness. A few months later, men of all parties fearlessly proclaimed his genius over the open grave, though some would never have ventured to do so, if they had not felt quite sure that he could not prepare any further shocks of surprise.

It is impossible to present a study of the experiences which caused the corrosive bitterness in Strindberg's attacks on everything and everybody, without reference to the unjust and Pharisaical criticism to which he had to submit. On the other hand, there can be no doubt that it was difficult to live with Strindberg. The Swedes had to live with him.

The many attacks made upon Strindberg in Sweden had one practical effect which caused him bitter disappointment. Theatrical managers fought shy of his plays. Fourteen years passed between the successful production of *The Father* in Paris and its performance in Stockholm. *Lady Julie* had to wait eighteen years before she was allowed to appear in Stockholm. In 1906 the play had a run of several weeks at " Folkteatern," in Stockholm, a playhouse for the working classes, where the aristocratic lady's downfall was appreciated in a crude, but whole-hearted manner.

The indifference shown in Sweden towards the performance of Strindberg's plays led him to plan a Strindberg-Theatre to be run on lines similar to those of the Théâtre Maeterlinck. After many diffi-culties the plan was at last realised in the autumn of 1907, when *The Intimate Theatre* began its stormy career with *The Pelican, The Burned Lot, Storm* and the Hoffmanesque and elliptic *Spook Sonata.* These plays were promptly attacked by critics who made little attempt to understand them.

The efforts made in certain quarters to silence Strindberg could not suppress the rising wave of admiration. When once the public had been brought in touch with him the anathema of the powerful literary coterie was useless. In 1901 Herr Albert Ranft had courageously staged *Gustavus Vasa* and *Erik XIV* at " Svenska Teatern " in Stockholm. They became theatrical successes. " Dramatiska Teatern " followed suit with *Charles XII, Easter* and *There are Crimes and Crimes.*

Strindberg writes an idiomatic Swedish which, in a sense, is not reproducible in another language. His sentences, whether in the dialogue of a drama, or in the story of a novel, are wrought with a nervous force which is untranslatable. His phrases seem to be innervated, warm-blooded entities, and support the theory that the sentence preceded the word in the evolution of speech. He is often ungrammatical; each sentence is a living whole which cannot be divided. Analyse him with syntax and dictionary, and you will find " mistakes " and startling neology.

The meaning will sometimes be obscure. But read him as you would listen to a piece of music with your ear to the harmonics, and you will find a consummate artist in words.

The rapidity of composition was probably to some extent responsible for the frequent repetitions of the same word within a short paragraph, the careless tautology of ideas, situations and episodes in his books. Many instances of such episode-repetition could be given. Thus *Comrades* and *Charles XII* contain similar phrases about the woman clipping the man's hair of strength, whilst his head rests in her lap. *The Dream Play* has several scenes which are " the doubles " of those related in *Fairhaven and Foulstrand*. A certain event connected with the tearing up of *The Swiss Family Robinson* serves the author's psychological purposes both in *To Damascus* and in *The Dream Play*. In *The Father* Laura secretly abstracts the contents of her husband's letter-bag, and in *To Damascus* " The Lady " is guilty of the same offence. Both in *Fairhaven and Foulstrand* and in *To Damascus* the woman promises not to read a certain book by the man which deals with his first marriage. She breaks the promise, and the disastrous effect is related with emphasis in both books. In *The Dance of Death* the remorseless Captain calmly refers to his attempt to drown his wife by pushing her into the water; the incident is more fully worked out in *Fairhaven and Foulstrand*, and is the theme of a story in *Fisher Folk*. Such repetitions cannot be attributed to poverty of imagination; they are the outcome of a too retentive emotional memory and an insistent need of expression, immediate expression.

It is curious to note that in spite of the richness and purity of his Swedish, in which the living tongue of the people is heard as never heretofore, there is not infrequently an admixture of foreign words and expressions. That his early verse-play *In Rome* should contain rhymes on "jouissance" and "connaissance," coupled with Swedish words, and that some of his early poems were adorned in the same manner is not surprising. But when Göran Persson in *Eric XIV* lightly throws out a hybrid drawing-room phrase: "*Tant mieux* for my enemies!" a jarring note is introduced which is difficult to explain in a dialogue, otherwise so carefully balanced. The habit of using root-words from many languages, to which he gave Swedish shape, grew upon Strindberg in later years. In the plays his characters suddenly begin to spout Latin and Greek, like the philosophic beggar in *To Damascus* and the sergeant-major in *Gustavus Adolphus*.

In 1901 Strindberg married Harriet Bosse, who had been the sympathetic interpreter on the stage of the women in some of his plays. The marriage was amicably dissolved in 1904. A little daughter of this marriage, Anne Marie, was very dear to his heart.

Poverty, the faithful companion of his youth, clung to him to the end. Even during the last years he was often in monetary difficulties; in his attacks upon the powers of the day he had no thought of what the morrow would bring to him. He had again and again to pay the penalty of speaking unpopular truths. And when money came his way he did not love it well enough to make it stay with him. He gave with a lavish, careless hand, with a heart ever warm for those who had less than he. When, on his last birthday, a purse containing 50,000 kronor had been presented to him, as a token of the people's love and admiration, he gave away large sums. When, at last, a great publisher bought the rights of all his published works in Sweden for some £11,000, the affluence came too late—for him.

When in January, 1912, the whole Swedish nation celebrated his sixty-third birthday it was nearly too late. The breath of death was already upon Strindberg as he stood on his balcony, waving his hand to the torchlight procession which passed the house, bending his head before the deafening cheers which rose from the multitudes, from whose lips the cry for August Strindberg rose in tones of jubilant hero-worship. As he stood there, raised above the bands and banners of the festive acclamation, it may be that the memories of past mistakes, past humiliation, and past struggle for goodness rose within that mighty brow, and kept pace with the steps of the marching crowd below. For he knew, as few have known, the comedy and the tragedy of life.

That night the theatres of Stockholm vied with each other in performing his plays. Laurel-wreathed busts and portraits of Strindberg were on view in the foyers and restaurants. The night came with public festivities in his honour, music and speeches of approbation.

But the dramatist remained at home in his Blue Tower with a few friends. The applause of the public touched his heart, but did not deceive him. He knew that the curtain was about to fall on his part in the perpetual performance in the Theatre of Life, and that new scenes were to follow, to be hissed and applauded until Time puts its last figure upon the stage.

On May 14, 1912, the stillness of death descended on the battlefield which was Strindberg's life. Siri von Essen had died three weeks before. Strindberg wept when his daughter Greta read the letter describing her passing. Then he left the room and came back dressed in black. He asked his daughter if the children would object to his sending a wreath to their mother's grave. She answered that it would give joy.

And at the funeral of Siri there lay on her coffin a wreath made of laurel and lilies, tied with white ribbon. There was no visible inscription, but the meaning seemed clear.

" Wipe out, and pass on ! "